More Slow Cooking

igloobooks

igloobooks

Published in 2016
by Igloo Books Ltd
Cottage Farm
Sywell
NN6 0BJ
www.igloobooks.com

Food photography and recipe development:
© Stockfood, The Food Media Agency
Cover image © Stockfood, The Food Media Agency

HUN001 0616
2 4 6 8 10 9 7 5 3
ISBN: 978-1-78557-532-7

Cover designed by Nicholas Gage
Interiors designed by Charles Wood-Penn
Edited by Caroline Icke

Printed and manufactured in China

Contents

Soups

Roasted Tomato Soup

SERVES 4

PREPARATION TIME 15 MINUTES

COOKING TIME 3 HOURS 15 MINUTES

INGREDIENTS

55 ml / 2 fl. oz / ¼ cup olive oil
2 cloves of garlic, minced
1 small onion, finely chopped
1 small carrot, peeled and finely diced
½ tsp dried basil
750 g / 1 lb 10 oz / 5 cups vine tomatoes, cored, seeded and roughly chopped
1 tbsp tomato purée
1 l / 1 pint 16 fl. oz / 4 cups vegetable stock
110 ml / 4 fl. oz / ½ cup double (heavy) cream
basil leaves, to garnish
salt and freshly ground black pepper

METHOD

1. Preheat the oven to 170°C (150°C fan) / 325F / gas 3.

2. Heat the olive oil in an ovenproof casserole dish set over a medium heat until hot, then add the garlic, onion, carrot and a little salt.

3. Cook for 5 minutes, stirring occasionally, until softened. Stir through the dried herbs and chopped tomatoes.

4. Move the vegetables to the oven to roast for 1 hour until very soft.

5. Remove from the oven and stir through the tomato purée, followed by the stock.

6. Pour into a slow cooker, cover with a lid and cook on high for 2 hours.

7. Blend with a stick blender until smooth. Stir through the cream and cook for a further 5 minutes, uncovered.

8. Adjust the seasoning to taste and ladle into bowls. Garnish with basil leaves before serving.

TOP TIP
Replace the cream with half-fat crème fraiche for a diet version.

French Onion Soup with Gruyère

SERVES 4

PREPARATION TIME 20 MINUTES

COOKING TIME 6 HOURS 10 MINUTES

INGREDIENTS

2 tbsp unsalted butter
2 tbsp sunflower oil
a few sprigs of thyme
2 cloves of garlic, crushed
6 large, brown onions, finely sliced
150 ml / 5 fl. oz / ⅔ cup dry white wine
1.25 l / 2 pints 4 fl. oz / 5 cups beef stock
½ baguette, cut into slices
150 g / 5 oz / 1 ½ cups Gruyère, grated
salt and freshly ground black pepper

METHOD

1. Heat together the butter and oil in a large, heavy-based saucepan set over a medium heat until hot.

2. Add the thyme, garlic, onions and a little salt, sweating for 5 minutes until starting to soften.

3. Deglaze the saucepan with white wine, reducing it by half. Cover with the stock and pour into a slow cooker.

4. Cover with a lid and cook on a low setting for 6 hours, stirring from time to time.

5. Preheat the grill to hot.

6. Adjust the seasoning of the soup to taste, then ladle into serving bowls.

7. Top with slices of baguette and a generous layer of Gruyère, then brown under the grill until the cheese is bubbling and turning golden brown.

8. Carefully remove from the grill and serve immediately.

TOP TIP
Remember to use heatproof bowls when serving this soup.

11

Curried Parsnip Soup

SERVES **4**

PREPARATION TIME **15 MINUTES**

COOKING TIME **5 HOURS 20 MINUTES**

INGREDIENTS

2 tbsp butter
1 tbsp vegetable oil
1 onion, finely chopped
500 g / 1 lb 2 oz / 3 ⅓ cups parsnips, peeled
    and diced
1 tsp ground cumin
1 tsp curry powder
900 ml / 1 pint 12 fl. oz / 4 cups vegetable stock
300 ml / 10 ½ fl. oz / 1 ⅓ cups whole milk
75 ml / 3 fl. oz / ⅓ cup double (heavy) cream
2 tbsp tarragon, finely chopped
salt and freshly ground black pepper

METHOD

1. Heat the butter and oil in a saucepan set over a medium heat until hot. Add the onion and sweat with a little salt for 5 minutes until softened.

2. Add the parsnips and spices and cook for 3 minutes, stirring occasionally. Add the stock, stir well and cook until simmering.

3. Pour the contents of the pan into a slow cooker. Cover and cook on low for 5 hours until the parsnips are tender.

4. Purée the soup in a food processor or using a stick blender until smooth.

5. Stir in the milk and return the soup to the slow cooker. Cook on high for 15 minutes until hot, then season to taste.

6. Ladle into soup bowls and top with a swirl of cream and sprinkle with chopped tarragon before serving.

TOP TIP
Use mild or hot curry powder to fit your tastes.

Red Lentil Soup

SERVES 4

PREPARATION TIME **15 MINUTES**

COOKING TIME **4 HOURS 15 MINUTES**

INGREDIENTS

55 ml / 2 fl. oz / ¼ cup sunflower oil
1 onion, finely sliced
2 cloves of garlic, chopped
5 cm (2 in) piece of root ginger, peeled
  and minced
1 red chilli (chili), seeded and finely chopped
2 tsp curry powder
1 tsp turmeric
300 g / 10 ½ oz / 1 ½ cups red lentils
200 g / 7 oz / 1 cup canned tomatoes, chopped
1 l / 1 pint 6 fl. oz / 4 cups vegetable stock
4 spring onions (scallions), sliced
1 small bunch of coriander (cilantro), chopped
salt and freshly ground black pepper

METHOD

1. Heat the oil in a saucepan and fry the onion until softened.

2. Add the garlic, ginger, chilli, curry powder and turmeric and cook for 2 minutes, then add the lentils and stir well.

3. Add the tomatoes and stock, season with salt and pepper and pour into a slow cooker.

4. Cover the cooker with a lid and cook on high for 4 hours until the lentils are soft. Adjust the seasoning to taste.

5. Serve garnished with the spring onions and coriander.

TOP TIP

Split yellow lentils, soaked in water overnight, are a good substitute.

Pea Soup

SERVES **4**

PREPARATION TIME **15 MINUTES**

COOKING TIME **5 HOURS 20 MINUTES**

INGREDIENTS

2 tbsp butter
1 onion, finely chopped
1 large potato, peeled and diced
½ tsp dried mint
450 g / 1 lb / 3 cups frozen petit pois, thawed
1 l / 1 pint 16 fl. oz / 4 cups vegetable stock
125 ml / 4 ½ fl. oz / ½ cup whole milk
salt and freshly ground black pepper

METHOD

1. Heat the butter in a saucepan set over a medium heat until hot. Add the onion, potato and a little salt, sweating for 7–8 minutes until softened.

2. Add the dried mint, stir well and add the peas. Cook for 2 minutes, stirring occasionally.

3. Add the stock, stir well and cook until simmering.

4. Pour the mixture into a slow cooker, then cover and cook on low for 5 hours, stirring occasionally.

5. Purée the soup in a food processor or using a stick blender until smooth.

6. Stir in the milk and return the soup to the slow cooker, cooking on high for 10 minutes until hot. Season to taste.

7. Ladle into soup bowls and garnish with more freshly ground black pepper before serving.

TOP TIP

If available, use fresh peas and reduce cooking time by 1 hour.

Carrot and Coriander Soup

SERVES 4

PREPARATION TIME 20 MINUTES

COOKING TIME 6 HOURS 20 MINUTES

INGREDIENTS

2 tbsp olive oil

1 large onion, finely chopped

1 tbsp ground coriander

750 g / 1 lb 10 oz / 5 cups carrots, peeled and chopped

1.25 l / 2 pints 4 fl. oz / 5 cups vegetable stock

150 ml / 5 fl. oz / ⅔ cup double (heavy) cream

1 small bunch of coriander (cilantro), roughly chopped

Salt and freshly ground black pepper

METHOD

1. Heat the olive oil in a large saucepan set over a medium heat until hot.

2. Add the onion and sweat with a little salt for 5 minutes, stirring occasionally, until soft.

3. Add the ground coriander and stir well, cooking for a further minute. Stir in the carrots, stir well and cover with the stock.

4. Pour into a slow cooker and cover with a lid. Cook on low for 6 hours until the carrot is very soft.

5. Blend with a stick blender or in a food processor until smooth.

6. Stir through the cream and cook on high for a further 10 minutes. Adjust the seasoning to taste and ladle into bowls.

7. Serve with a garnish of chopped coriander.

TOP TIP

A squeeze of fresh lime juice just before serving adds a little acidity.

Summer Minestrone

SERVES 4

PREPARATION TIME 20 MINUTES

COOKING TIME 6 HOURS 30 MINUTES

INGREDIENTS

55 ml / 2 fl. oz / ¼ cup olive oil
½ white cabbage, shredded
2 potatoes, peeled and diced
2 cloves of garlic, minced
2 large carrots, peeled and diced
2 large sticks of celery, diced
1 bay leaf
400 g / 14 oz / 2 cups passata
1 l / 1 pint 16 fl. oz / 4 cups vegetable stock
150 g / 5 oz / 1 ½ cups ditalini pasta
2 tbsp basil leaves, finely chopped
55 g / 2 oz / ½ cup Parmesan, shaved
salt and freshly ground black pepper

METHOD

1. Heat the olive oil in a casserole dish set over a medium heat until hot.

2. Sweat the cabbage, potatoes, garlic, carrot, celery and bay leaf with a little salt for 8–10 minutes until they start to soften.

3. Stir through passata and stock, cooking until simmering.

4. Pour the soup into a slow cooker, cover and cook on low for 6 hours until the vegetables are tender.

5. Discard the bay leaf and stir through the ditalini. Cook, uncovered, on a higher setting for 10–15 minutes until the pasta is tender.

6. Stir through the chopped basil and season to taste. Ladle into bowls and garnish with shaved Parmesan.

TOP TIP
If possible, use a fresh bay leaf for best results.

White Bean Soup

SERVES 4

PREPARATION TIME 15 MINUTES

COOKING TIME 6 HOURS 15 MINUTES

INGREDIENTS

2 tbsp olive oil
1 large onion, chopped
2 carrots, peeled and sliced
2 large potatoes, peeled and roughly chopped
400 g / 14 oz / 2 cups canned white beans,
    drained
1.25 l / 2 pints 4 fl. oz / 5 cups vegetable stock
2 vine tomatoes, cored, seeded and sliced
2 tbsp flat-leaf parsley, chopped
salt and freshly ground black pepper

METHOD

1. Heat the oil in a large saucepan set over a medium heat until hot. Add the onion, carrot, potato and a little salt, sweating for 7–8 minutes until softened.

2. Add the beans and stock, stir well and cook until simmering.

3. Pour into a slow cooker and cover with a lid. Cook on a low setting for 5–6 hours until the beans are very tender.

4. Stir through the tomatoes and adjust the seasoning to taste.

5. Ladle into bowls, garnish with a sprinkle of parsley and serve with a little more ground black pepper on top.

TOP
TIP
Add a couple of handfuls of chopped kale for an enhanced taste.

Mushroom Soup

SERVES 4

PREPARATION TIME 15 MINUTES

COOKING TIME 7 HOURS 20 MINUTES

INGREDIENTS

2 tbsp olive oil
1 tbsp butter
1 onion, finely chopped
450 g / 1 lb / 6 cups button mushrooms, brushed
    clean and chopped
a few sprigs of thyme
1 l / 1 pint 16 fl. oz / 4 cups vegetable stock
175 ml / 6 fl. oz / ¾ cup double (heavy) cream
a few chives
a few sprigs of flat-leaf parsley
salt and freshly ground black pepper

METHOD

1. Heat together the oil and butter in a large saucepan.

2. Add the onion, mushrooms and a pinch of salt. Fry for 5 minutes, stirring occasionally.

3. Add the thyme, stir well and cover with the stock. Pour into a slow cooker and cover with a lid.

4. Cook on low for 6–7 hours until the mushrooms are very soft.

5. Add the cream and cook on high for around 10 minutes, then purée with a stick blender until smooth.

6. Season to taste with salt and pepper, then ladle into bowls and serve with a garnish of the herbs on top.

TOP TIP

Make sure that the soup doesn't approach boiling point after adding the cream.

Corn Chowder

SERVES 4

PREPARATION TIME 20 MINUTES

COOKING TIME 6 HOURS 30 MINUTES

INGREDIENTS

2 tbsp butter
150 g / 5 oz / 1 cup pancetta lardons
1 large onion, finely chopped
2 cloves of garlic, minced
4 medium floury potatoes, peeled and diced
a sprig of thyme, leaves stripped
500 ml / 18 fl. oz / 2 cups whole milk
750 ml / 1 pint 6 fl. oz / 3 cups ham stock
400 g / 14 oz / 2 cups canned sweetcorn, drained
100 ml / 3 ½ fl. oz / ½ cup double (heavy) cream
2 tbsp flat-leaf parsley, chopped
salt and freshly ground black pepper

METHOD

1. Heat the butter in a large saucepan set over a medium heat until hot.

2. Add the pancetta and fry for 4–5 minutes until golden, then remove half of the pancetta and reserve for later.

3. Add the onion, garlic, potatoes and thyme. Stir well and cook for a further 6–7 minutes until the vegetables are softened.

4. Cover with the milk and stock, cooking until simmering. Pour into a slow cooker and cover with a lid.

5. Cook on low for 6 hours, until the potatoes are very tender. Blend with a stick blender or in a food processor until smooth, then return the soup to the slow cooker.

6. Add the corn and cream and reserved pancetta, stirring well. Cook on high for 15 minutes. Season to taste with salt and pepper.

7. Ladle into bowls and garnish with a little chopped parsley before serving.

TOP TIP
Leave the chowder unblended for a more rustic version.

Spicy Sausage and Tomato Soup

SERVES 4

PREPARATION TIME 15 MINUTES

COOKING TIME 5 HOURS 20 MINUTES

INGREDIENTS

2 tbsp olive oil
2 cloves of garlic, minced
300 g / 10 ½ oz / 2 cups chorizo, peeled and sliced
1 tsp paprika
400 g / 14 oz / 2 cups canned white beans
400 g / 14 oz / 2 cups passata
1 l / 1 pint 16 fl. oz / 4 cups vegetable stock
2 tbsp basil leaves, chopped
crusty white bread, to serve
salt and freshly ground black pepper

METHOD

1. Heat the oil in a large saucepan set over a medium heat until hot. Add the garlic and a little salt, frying for 2 minutes.

2. Add the chorizo and paprika and continue to cook for 3–4 minutes, stirring frequently. Stir in the beans, passata and vegetable stock.

3. Cook until simmering, then pour into a slow cooker. Cover with a lid and cook on a low setting for 5 hours until the beans are tender.

4. Adjust the seasoning of the soup with salt and pepper.

5. Ladle into bowls, garnish with chopped basil and serve with crusty white bread on the side.

TOP TIP

Omit the chorizo for a vegetarian version of this soup.

Sweet Potato and Black Bean Soup

SERVES 4

PREPARATION TIME 20 MINUTES

COOKING TIME 7 HOURS 30 MINUTES

INGREDIENTS

1 tbsp olive oil
1 onion, finely chopped
2 cloves of garlic, minced
1 tsp paprika
½ tsp ground cumin
½ tsp dried oregano
a pinch of cayenne pepper
900 g / 2 lb / 6 cups sweet potatoes, peeled
    and diced
200 g / 7 oz / 1 cup passata
1.25 l / 2 pint 4 fl. oz / 5 cups vegetable stock
400 g / 14 oz / 2 cups canned black beans
200 g / 7 oz / 1 cup canned sweetcorn, drained
1 large, red chilli (chili), seeded and sliced
1 lime, cut into wedges
salt and freshly ground black pepper

METHOD

1. Heat the olive oil in a large saucepan set over a medium heat until hot.

2. Add the onion, garlic and a pinch of salt and sweat for 5 minutes until softened. Add the ground spices and herbs, stir well and cook for a further minute.

3. Add the sweet potato, then stir in the passata and stock.

4. Pour everything into a slow cooker, then cover the cooker with a lid and cook on low for 6–7 hours until the sweet potato is soft.

5. Once soft, pulse the soup with a stick blender, until the soup is smooth with a little texture. Add the beans, sweetcorn and chilli on top and cover the pot with a lid.

6. Cook on high for 15 minutes, then adjust the seasoning to taste, ladle into bowls and serve with wedges of lime.

TOP TIP

Remember to stir the soup from time to time when in the slow cooker.

Thai Coconut Chicken Soup

SERVES 4

PREPARATION TIME **15 MINUTES**

COOKING TIME **5 HOURS 20 MINUTES**

INGREDIENTS

2 tbsp groundnut oil
1 tbsp green curry paste
1 large carrot, peeled and cut into thin batons
200 g / 7 oz / 1 cup canned bamboo shoots, drained
2 large, skinless chicken breasts, diced
750 ml / 1 pint 16 fl. oz / 3 cups chicken stock
400 ml / 14 fl. oz / 1 ⅔ cups coconut milk
1–2 tbsp fish sauce
1–2 tbsp rice wine vinegar
1 tbsp soft light brown sugar
1–2 tbsp light soy sauce
110 g / 4 oz / ⅔ cup mangetout
250 g / 9 oz / 2 cups cooked jasmine rice
1 red chilli (chili), sliced
a small handful of Thai basil leaves

METHOD

1. Heat the oil in a large saucepan set over a medium heat until hot. Stir in the curry paste and fry in the oil for 1 minute.

2. Add the carrot, bamboo and chicken to the pan. Cook for a further minute, then cover with the stock and coconut milk.

3. Cook until simmering, then pour into a slow cooker. Cover with a lid and cook on a low setting for 5 hours until the chicken is cooked through and tender.

4. Season the broth with fish sauce, rice wine vinegar, sugar and soy sauce to taste.

5. Add the mangetout and cook for a further 5 minutes, then ladle into bowls. Serve with rice, sliced red chilli and a few basil leaves.

TOP TIP
For a more pronounced chicken taste, use chicken thighs instead of breasts.

Lemon and Chicken Rice Soup

SERVES 4

PREPARATION TIME 15 MINUTES

COOKING TIME 5 HOURS 15 MINUTES

INGREDIENTS

1 tbsp sunflower oil
2 large, skinless chicken breasts, diced
175 g / 6 oz / 1 cup long grain white rice,
    rinsed thoroughly
1.25 l / 2 pints 4 fl. oz / 5 cups chicken stock
2 lemons
1 small handful of flat-leaf parsley, chopped
salt and freshly ground black pepper

METHOD

1. Heat the oil in a saucepan set over a medium heat until hot.

2. Add the chicken and a little seasoning, then cook for 3–4 minutes until starting to brown.

3. Stir in the rice, cover with the stock and cook until simmering. Add the juice of one lemon and stir well.

4. Pour into a slow cooker, cover with a lid and cook on low for 5 hours until the rice has absorbed some of the stock and the chicken is cooked through.

5. Season the soup with salt and pepper, then ladle into bowls and garnish with parsley.

6. Cut the remaining lemon into thin slices and use as a garnish.

TOP TIP

If the soup starts to run dry, add a little stock or hot water to the slow cooker.

Fish Chowder

SERVES 4

PREPARATION TIME 20 MINUTES

COOKING TIME 6 HOURS 30 MINUTES

INGREDIENTS

2 tbsp butter
1 large onion, finely chopped
2 cloves of garlic, minced
4 medium floury potatoes, peeled and diced
1 tsp mild curry powder
500 ml / 18 fl. oz / 2 cups whole milk
750 ml / 1 pint 6 fl. oz / 3 cups fish stock
1 courgette (zucchini), diced
100 ml / 3 ½ fl. oz / ½ cup double (heavy) cream
450 g / 1 lb / 3 cups skinless cod fillet, pin-boned
    and diced
4 rashers of streaky bacon
a few sprigs of thyme
salt and freshly ground black pepper

METHOD

1. Heat the butter in a large saucepan set over a medium heat until hot. Add the onion, garlic and potato and fry for 6–7 minutes until softened.

2. Stir in the curry powder and cook for 1 minute, stirring well.

3. Cover with the milk and stock, cooking until simmering. Pour into a slow cooker and cover with a lid.

4. Cook on low for 6 hours or until the potatoes are very tender. Blend with a stick blender or in a food processor until smooth, then return the soup to the slow cooker.

5. Add the courgette, cream and cod, stirring well. Cook on high for 15 minutes, then season to taste with salt and pepper.

6. Meanwhile, heat the grill to hot and grill the bacon for 2–3 minutes on both sides until golden and crisp. Remove from the grill and drain on kitchen paper, breaking into pieces once cool enough to handle.

7. Ladle the soup into bowls and garnish with thyme and bacon before serving.

TOP TIP
The cod will be ready when it flakes easily with a fork and appears opaque.

Poultry

Roast Chicken

SERVES *4*

PREPARATION TIME *20–25* MINUTES

COOKING TIME *1 HOUR 25* MINUTES

INGREDIENTS

1.6 kg / 3 ½ lb chicken, cleaned with wishbone
    removed, legs trussed

1 lemon, halved

1 head of garlic, split in half

55 g / 2 oz / ¼ cup butter, softened

2 medium onions, roughly sliced

2 tbsp olive oil

2 sprigs of rosemary

a small bunch of oregano, torn

a sprig of bay leaves

flaked sea salt and freshly ground black pepper

METHOD

1. Preheat the oven to 180°C (160°C fan) /
   350F / gas 4 and line a roasting tray with
   greaseproof paper.

2. Stuff the cavity of the bird with half a lemon
   and half the head of garlic. Season the
   insides with salt and pepper, then rub the
   chicken with the softened butter.

3. Roughly chop some of the remaining garlic
   cloves and rub into the crown of the chicken

4. Position the remaining garlic, lemon and the
   onion on the tray and drizzle with olive oil.
   Sit the chicken on top and roast for 1 hour
   15–25 minutes until golden all over.

5. To check that the chicken is cooked, pierce
   the thickest part of the thigh; if the juices
   run clear, it is ready. Alternatively, check
   with a meat thermometer; if the thigh
   registers at least 70°C / 160F, it is ready.

6. Remove from the oven and rest, covered
   loosely with kitchen foil, for 10 minutes.

7. Garnish the chicken with the herbs and
   a little more salt and pepper to serve.

TOP TIP

Ask your butcher to
remove the wishbone
and truss the legs if
you need help.

One Pot Chicken Pie

SERVES 4

PREPARATION TIME 15 MINUTES

COOKING TIME 1 HOUR 45 MINUTES

INGREDIENTS

tbsp sunflower oil

tbsp butter

medium carrots, peeled and sliced

large onion, chopped

large, skinless chicken breasts, diced

00 ml / 18 fl. oz / 2 cups chicken stock

tbsp cornflour (cornstarch)

tbsp whole milk

25 g / 8 oz / 2 cups fresh peas

small handful of flat-leaf parsley,
   finely chopped

00 g / 7 oz ready-made puff pastry

little plain (all-purpose) flour, for dusting

egg yolk, beaten

tbsp sesame seeds

alt and freshly ground black pepper

METHOD

1. Heat together the oil and butter in a casserole dish set over a medium heat until hot.

2. Add the carrots, onion and a little salt, and sweat for 5 minutes until starting to soften. Add the chicken, stir well and cook for a further 5 minutes until starting to brown.

3. Cover the mixture with the chicken stock and cook until simmering. Cook steadily for 10 minutes until slightly thickened.

4. Whisk together the cornflour and milk to make a paste. Whisk the paste into the gravy to thicken, making sure the gravy is simmering.

5. Stir through the peas and parsley, then season to taste with salt and pepper.

6. Preheat the oven to 170°C (150°C fan) / 325F / gas 3. Spoon the filling into a 900 g / 2 lb round pie dish.

7. Roll out the pastry on a lightly floured surface to a round about 0.5 cm (¼ in) thick and the same size as the pie dish.

8. Drape the pastry over the filling, sealing it against the inside of the rim of the pie dish. Brush with the egg yolk and sprinkle over the sesame seeds.

9. Bake for 1 hour 5–10 minutes until golden and puffed before serving.

TOP TIP

Frozen peas are fine to use if fresh are not available.

Chicken Korma

SERVES 4

PREPARATION TIME 20 MINUTES

COOKING TIME 5 HOURS 15 MINUTES

INGREDIENTS

2 medium onions, chopped
4 cloves of garlic, peeled
5 cm (2 in) piece of root ginger, peeled
55 ml / 2 fl. oz / ¼ cup sunflower oil
a pinch ground cardamom
2 tsp ground cumin
2 tsp ground coriander
1 tsp ground turmeric
3 large, skinless chicken breasts, diced
2 curry leaves
4 lime leaves
500 ml / 18 fl. oz / 2 cups chicken stock
200 ml / 7 fl. oz / 1 cup coconut milk
75 g / 3 oz / ¾ cup ground almonds
150 g / 5 oz / ⅔ cup coconut yogurt
2 red chillies (chilies), sliced
a stick of celery, finely diced
salt and freshly ground black pepper

METHOD

1. Blend together the onion, garlic and ginger in a food processor until paste-like.

2. Heat the oil in a large saucepan set over a moderate heat until hot. Add the paste and a pinch of salt, frying for 3 minutes until turning golden.

3. Add the ground spices, stir well and cook over a reduced heat for 1 minute, then stir in the chicken and the curry and lime leaves.

4. Cover with the stock and coconut milk, then stir through the ground almonds. Spoon the contents of the pan into a slow cooker.

5. Cover with a lid and cook on low for 5 hours until the chicken is tender.

6. Stir through the coconut yogurt to thicken the sauce. Adjust the seasoning to taste and stir through the sliced chillies, cooking uncovered for a further 5 minutes.

7. Ladle into bowls before serving, scattered with diced celery.

TOP TIP
Remove the ground almonds for a nut-free version.

Coq au Vin

ERVES 4

REPARATION TIME **20 MINUTES**

OOKING TIME **2 HOURS 20 MINUTES**

INGREDIENTS

0 g / 3 ½ oz / ⅔ cup pancetta lardons

bsp olive oil

bsp unsalted butter

chicken legs, trimmed

sp herbes de Provence

cloves of garlic, lightly crushed

bay leaves

bouquet garni

0 ml / 1 pint 6 fl. oz / 3 cups red wine

0 ml / 1 pint 6 fl. oz / 3 cups chicken stock

0 g / 10 ½ oz / 2 cups cherry tomatoes on
the vine

lt and freshly ground black pepper

METHOD

1. Heat a casserole dish over a moderate heat
   until hot. Preheat the oven to 170°C (150°C
   fan) / 325F / gas 3.

2. Add the pancetta and fry for 3–4 minutes
   until golden, then remove from the pan and
   add the olive oil and butter.

3. Season the chicken legs with the herbes de
   Provence, salt and pepper. Brown in the oil
   and butter, turning once, then add the garlic,
   bay leaves, bouquet garni and pancetta.

4. Cover the chicken with the red wine and
   stock. Cook until simmering, then add the
   cherry tomatoes.

5. Transfer the dish to the oven to cook for
   2 hours until the chicken is cooked through.

6. Remove from the oven and season to taste
   before serving.

TOP TIP

Move the chicken
pieces around from
time to time to ensure
even cooking.

Spicy Chicken Noodles

SERVES 4

PREPARATION TIME **15 MINUTES**

COOKING TIME **3 HOURS 20 MINUTES**

INGREDIENTS

2 tbsp sesame oil
2 dried red chillies (chilies)
2 large, skinless chicken breasts, diced
1 l / 1 pint 16 fl. oz / 4 cups chicken stock
350 g / 12 oz / 3 cups thin egg noodles
250 g / 9 oz / 2 cups green (string) beans, trimmed
150 g / 5 oz / 1 ½ cups baby sweetcorn, sliced
2–3 tbsp soy sauce
2–3 tbsp rice wine vinegar
1 tbsp black sesame seeds
1 tbsp white sesame seeds
a pinch of chilli (chili) powder
4 spring onions (scallions), sliced
freshly ground pepper

METHOD

1. Heat the oil in a large saucepan or casserole dish set over a medium heat until hot.

2. Add the chillies and fry for 1 minute. Add the chicken breasts and brown lightly in the oil.

3. Cover with the stock and cook until simmering.

4. Place the noodles in a slow cooker, pour over the contents of the saucepan, then cover with a lid and cook on a low setting for 2 hours.

5. After 2 hours, remove the lid and add the beans and sweetcorn. Cover and cook for a further hour until the vegetables are tender and the noodles are soft.

6. Season to taste with soy sauce, rice wine vinegar and pepper. Lift the noodles and soup into bowls.

7. Cut the chicken into slices and lay on top of the noodles, garnish with sesame seeds and chilli powder. Sprinkle over the spring onions before serving.

TOP TIP
The chicken can be replaced with sirloin or rib-eye steak.

Chicken and Chorizo Paella

SERVES 4

PREPARATION TIME 20 MINUTES

COOKING TIME 5 HOURS 20 MINUTES

INGREDIENTS

tbsp olive oil
250 g / 9 oz piece of chorizo, peeled and sliced
chicken thighs, trimmed and scored
large onion, chopped
cloves of garlic, minced
large red peppers, sliced
250 g / 9 oz / 1 ⅓ cups paella rice
pinch of saffron threads, infused in the stock
700 ml / 1 pint 2 fl. oz / 2 ½ cups chicken stock
small vine tomatoes, cored, seeded and diced
250 g / 9 oz / 2 cups fresh peas
few sprigs of dill, chopped
lemon, cut into wedges
salt and freshly ground black pepper

METHOD

1. Heat the oil in a casserole dish set over a moderate heat until hot. Add the chorizo and fry for 3 minutes until golden.

2. Remove from the dish and drain on kitchen paper. Season the chicken thighs with salt and pepper, then brown in the oil.

3. Add the onion, garlic, red peppers and chorizo to the dish. Fry for a further 2 minutes, then stir in the rice.

4. Cover with the infused stock and stir well. Cook until simmering, then transfer the contents of the dish to a slow cooker.

5. Cover and cook on a low setting for 5 hours until the rice is tender.

6. Stir through the tomatoes and peas and cook uncovered for a further 10 minutes.

7. Season to taste with salt and pepper, then serve with a sprinkle of chopped dill and the lemon wedges on the side.

TOP TIP

Use extra vegetables and vegetable stock to make this dish vegetarian.

Chicken Casserole

SERVES 4

PREPARATION TIME 20 MINUTES

COOKING TIME 1 HOUR 50 MINUTES

INGREDIENTS

1 medium chicken, jointed into 8 pieces
55 ml / 2 fl. oz / ¼ cup olive oil
a small bunch of thyme
2 tbsp tarragon, chopped
2 bay leaves
2 cloves of garlic, finely chopped
750 ml / 1 pint 6 fl. oz / 3 cups chicken stock
8 spring onions (scallions), trimmed
250 g / 9 oz / 2 cups green asparagus, trimmed
    and chopped
200 g / 7 oz / 2 cups small carrots, peeled
450 g / 1 lb / 3 cups new potatoes, scrubbed clean
salt and freshly ground black pepper

METHOD

1. Preheat the oven to 170°C (150°C fan) / 325F / gas 3.

2. Season the chicken pieces with salt and pepper and heat the oil in a large casserole dish set over a moderate heat until hot.

3. Seal the chicken in the oil, browning well all over. Reduce the heat under the dish a little.

4. Add the thyme, tarragon, bay leaves and garlic, stirring well. Cover with the stock and cook until simmering.

5. Add the vegetables to the dish, then transfer the contents of the dish to a roasting dish.

6. Cook for 1 hour 20–30 minutes until the chicken is golden and cooked through, and the vegetables are tender.

7. Remove from the oven and leave to stand for 5 minutes before serving.

TOP TIP

Pat dry the pieces of chicken with kitchen paper, then season and seal.

Thai Green Chicken Curry

SERVES 4

PREPARATION TIME **15 MINUTES**

COOKING TIME **3 HOURS 25 MINUTES**

INGREDIENTS

tbsp groundnut oil

shallots, finely chopped

tbsp Thai green curry paste

skinless chicken thighs, diced

00 ml / 14 fl. oz / 1 ²/₃ cups coconut milk

00 ml / 14 fl. oz / 1 ²/₃ cups chicken stock

tbsp fish sauce

tbsp soft light brown sugar

lime, juiced

large handful of pea aubergines (eggplants)

large, red chillies (chilies), sliced

small bunch of Thai basil, leaves picked

alt and freshly ground black pepper

METHOD

1. Heat the oil in a saucepan set over a moderate heat until hot. Add the shallot and paste, then fry for 2 minutes.

2. Add the chicken and continue to cook for a further 3 minutes, stirring occasionally. Cover with the coconut milk and stock, then simmer. Pour into a slow cooker.

3. Cover with a lid and cook on a medium setting for 3 hours until the chicken is tender and cooked through.

4. Stir through the fish sauce, sugar, lime juice and pea aubergines and cook for a further 15 minutes until thickened.

5. Adjust the seasoning to taste and ladle into serving bowls. Garnish with sliced red chillies and Thai basil leaves.

TOP TIP

For those allergic to groundnut oil, use sunflower oil.

Teriyaki Chicken Kebabs

SERVES 4

PREPARATION TIME 45 MINUTES

COOKING TIME 3 HOURS 10 MINUTES

INGREDIENTS

2 large, skinless chicken breasts, cubed
4 spring onions (scallions), trimmed and halved
100 ml / 3 ½ fl. oz / ½ cup water
55 ml / 2 fl. oz / ¼ cup dark soy sauce
2 tbsp mirin
1 tbsp rice wine vinegar
2 tsp honey
1 tbsp chilli (chili) sauce
a small bunch of flat-leaf parsley
a small handful of mixed leaf salad
salt and freshly ground black pepper

METHOD

1. Soak four bamboo skewers in water for 30 minutes.

2. Thread the chicken onto the skewers, alternating with pieces of spring onion.

3. Sit in a slow cooker, cover with a lid and cook on a high heat for 3 hours.

4. Meanwhile, combine the water, soy sauce, mirin, rice wine vinegar, honey and chilli sauce in a saucepan.

5. Warm over a low heat until combined. Season to taste with salt and pepper and set to one side.

6. Once the chicken is cooked, preheat the grill to hot.

7. Brush the chicken with the sauce and grill for 1–2 minutes on both sides, until glazed.

8. Serve with parsley and salad on the side.

TOP TIP

Turkey breast makes for a leaner alternative to chicken in this recipe.

Slow-cooked Duck Legs

ERVES 4

REPARATION TIME 15 MINUTES

OOKING TIME 8 HOURS 30 MINUTES

INGREDIENTS

- bsp sunflower oil
- duck legs, trimmed
- 0 ml / 1 pint 9 fl. oz / 3 ½ cups chicken stock, hot
- 5 g / 6 oz / 1 cup couscous
- g / 3 oz / ¾ cup pine nuts
- g / 2 oz / ⅓ cup raisins
- bsp olive oil
- tsp cumin seeds
- eaches, pitted and sliced
- lt and freshly ground black pepper

METHOD

1. Heat the oil in a large casserole dish set over a moderate heat until hot. Season the duck legs with salt and pepper, then seal in the hot oil.

2. Remove from the dish once golden on both sides and place in a slow cooker. Pour in half of the stock and cover the cooker with a lid.

3. Cook on low for 8 hours until the meat comes away easily from the bone.

4. Place the couscous, pine nuts and raisins in a mixing bowl. Pour over the remaining hot chicken stock, stir once, then cover the bowl with cling film.

5. Leave the couscous to absorb the stock for 10 minutes.

6. Meanwhile, heat the olive oil in a frying pan, add the cumin seeds and fry for 30 seconds. Add the peach slices and a little seasoning.

7. Sauté for 4–5 minutes, turning occasionally, until golden and lightly charred.

8. Fluff the couscous with a fork and pile onto plates. Top with the duck legs and any juice from the slow cooker. Serve with the peaches on the sides.

TOP TIP

Turn the duck legs after 4 hours in the slow cooker.

Fruity Roasted Duck

SERVES 4

PREPARATION TIME 10 MINUTES

COOKING TIME 2 HOURS 15 MINUTES

INGREDIENTS

2 large duck legs, trimmed and cleaned
2 tbsp olive oil
2 nectarines, pitted and chopped
350 g / 12 oz / 2 ⅓ cups dried prunes
a small bunch of thyme
2 bay leaves
salt and freshly ground black pepper

METHOD

1. Preheat the oven to 150°C (130°C fan) / 300F / gas 2. Season the duck legs with salt and pepper.

2. Place a large frying pan over a low heat and place the duck legs, meat-side down, in the pan.

3. Fry for 5 minutes until the skin starts to turn golden.

4. Arrange the nectarine and prunes in a roasting tray. Tuck the duck legs in and around the fruit and drizzle with olive oil and any rendered fat from the pan.

5. Roast for 2 hours until the duck legs are golden and tender.

6. Remove from the oven and garnish with herbs before serving.

TOP TIP
Flip the duck legs halfway through roasting for best results.

Pot-roasted Pheasant

SERVES 6

PREPARATION TIME 20 MINUTES

COOKING TIME 2 HOURS 25 MINUTES

INGREDIENTS

small pheasants, cleaned and trussed
g / 2 oz / ¼ cup butter, softened
0 g / 5 oz / 1 cup pancetta lardons
5 g / 8 oz / 3 cups button mushrooms, brushed clean
mall shallots, peeled
ticks of celery, chopped
5 ml / 4 ½ fl. oz / ½ cup dry white wine
0 ml / 18 fl. oz / 2 cups chicken stock
prigs of thyme
mall handful of oregano, chopped
t and freshly ground black pepper

METHOD

1. Preheat the oven to 170°C (150°C fan) / 325F / gas 3.

2. Rub the pheasants with butter and season their insides and outsides with salt and pepper.

3. Heat a casserole dish over a moderate heat until hot. Seal the pheasants in the dish until golden all over, then remove from the dish to one side.

4. Add the pancetta and fry for 3–4 minutes. Add the mushrooms, shallots and celery and continue to fry for 5 minutes, stirring occasionally.

5. Deglaze the pan with the wine, scraping the base well. Reduce the heat a little and sit the pheasants back in the dish on top of the vegetables.

6. Pour in the stock and tuck in the thyme sprigs. Season with salt and pepper and move the dish to the oven.

7. Roast for 1 hour 45–55 minutes until the pheasants are cooked through and golden.

8. Remove from the oven and leave to rest for 10 minutes before serving with a garnish of chopped oregano.

TOP TIP

Singe any feathers or hair from the pheasants using a chef's blowtorch.

63

Slow-roasted Turkey

SERVES *8*

PREPARATION TIME *20 MINUTES*

COOKING TIME *4 HOURS 40 MINUTES*

INGREDIENTS

3.5 kg / 8 lb turkey, cleaned and trimmed
110 g / 4 oz / ½ cup clarified butter
3 heads of garlic, split in half
1 bouquet garni
2 white onions, split in half
2 parsnips, peeled and chopped
salt and freshly ground black pepper

METHOD

1. Preheat the oven to 170°C (150°C fan) / 325F / gas 3.

2. Rub the turkey with half of the clarified butter. Season the inside and outside with plenty of salt and pepper, then stuff with some of the garlic and a bouquet garni.

3. Arrange the remaining garlic in a large roasting tray and mix with the onions and parsnips, then drizzle with the remaining clarified butter and season well with salt and pepper.

4. Roast the turkey for 4 hours until the thickest part of the thigh registers at least 71°C / 160F on a meat thermometer.

5. Remove from the oven, cover loosely with kitchen foil and leave to rest for at least 30 minutes before serving.

TOP TIP
The turkey can be left to rest for up to 1 hour before carving if needed.

Stuffed Turkey

RVES 8

EPARATION TIME 25 MINUTES

OKING TIME 2 HOURS 25 MINUTES

GREDIENTS

g / 11 lb turkey crown, butterflied

arge skinless duck breast, trimmed

0 g / 1 lb / 3 cups sausage meat

arge Granny Smith apple, peeled, cored
and diced

0 g / 3 ½ oz / ⅔ cup raspberries

sp thyme

mall bunch of sage

g / 2 oz / ¼ cup butter, melted

ed onions, sliced

ellow courgette (zucchini), sliced

ourgette (zucchini), sliced

0 g / 9 oz / 2 cups asparagus, woody
ends removed

0 g / 9 oz / 2 cups mangetout

ml / 2 fl. oz / ¼ cup olive oil

osp flat-leaf parsley, finely chopped

t and freshly ground black pepper

METHOD

1. Preheat the oven to 220°C (200°C fan) / 425F / gas 7.

2. Open up the turkey crown and season with salt and pepper. Pound out the duck breast with a meat tenderizer, then lay down in the centre of the turkey.

3. Mix together the sausage meat, apple, raspberries, thyme and a few chopped sage leaves in a mixing bowl and season.

4. Spoon the stuffing over the duck breast and spread it out evenly. Bring the sides of the turkey breast up and around the stuffing and tie securely with kitchen string.

5. Brush the stuffed crown with melted butter and season with salt and pepper. Sit in a roasting tray.

6. Roast for 30 minutes, then reduce the oven to 170°C (150°C fan) / 325F / gas 3. Roast for a further 1 hour 15–25 minutes until the inside of the crown registers at least 74°C / 165F on a meat thermometer.

7. Remove from the roasting tray, transfer to a platter and cover tightly with kitchen foil.

8. Combine the vegetables in the roasting tray and toss with the olive oil and some seasoning. Roast for 25–30 minutes until tender.

9. Sprinkle the turkey crown with chopped parsley and serve with the roast vegetables and remaining sage.

TOP TIP

Trim any excess fat or skin from the turkey before butterflying.

Beef, Pork and Lamb

Boeuf Bourguignon

SERVES 4

PREPARATION TIME 20–25 MINUTES

COOKING TIME 7 HOURS 30 MINUTES

INGREDIENTS

75 ml / 3 fl. oz / ⅓ cup sunflower oil
900 g / 2 lb / 6 cups chuck steak, trimmed
    and cubed
150 g / 5 oz / 1 cup pancetta lardons
8 shallots, quartered
300 g / 10 ½ oz / 4 cups button mushrooms,
    brushed clean
2 cloves of garlic, chopped
2 tbsp plain (all-purpose) flour
750 ml / 1 pint 16 fl. oz / 3 cups red wine
2 bay leaves
500 ml / 18 fl. oz / 2 cups beef stock
2 tbsp flat-leaf parsley, chopped
salt and freshly ground black pepper

METHOD

1. Heat a little oil in a casserole dish set over
   a moderate heat until hot. Season the beef
   and seal in batches, using a little fresh oil
   for each batch.

2. Add the pancetta, shallots, mushrooms and
   garlic and fry for 2 minutes. Add the flour,
   stir well and cook for 1 minute.

3. Deglaze the dish with a little red wine,
   allowing it to reduce by half, then add
   the remainder.

4. Stir in the bay leaves and stock, then pour
   everything into a slow cooker.

5. Cover and cook on low for 7 hours until
   the beef is tender and pulls away between
   your fingers.

6. Season to taste with and serve with a
   garnish of chopped parsley.

TOP TIP
Give the stew a stir
from time to time
during cooking.

Beef Rendang

SERVES 4

PREPARATION TIME 15–20 MINUTES

COOKING TIME 6 HOURS 40 MINUTES

INGREDIENTS

75 ml / 3 fl. oz / ⅓ cup sunflower oil

1 tsp cloves

1 tsp ground cinnamon

5 shallots, chopped

2 Thai red chillies (chilies)

5 cm (2 in) piece of root ginger, peeled and chopped

2 tbsp macadamia nuts

900 g / 2 lb / 6 cups chuck steak, trimmed and cubed

350 ml / 12 fl. oz / 1 ½ cups beef stock

150 ml / 5 fl. oz / ⅔ cup coconut milk

2 tbsp lime leaves

1 small bunch of coriander (cilantro), chopped

Salt and freshly ground black pepper

METHOD

1. Blend 2 tbsp of oil with the cloves, cinnamon, shallots, chillies, ginger, macadamia nuts and seasoning in a food processor until smooth.

2. Heat a little of the remaining oil in a casserole dish set over a moderate heat until hot. Season the beef and seal in batches, using a little fresh oil each time, until golden all over.

3. Remove the beef from the dish and add the prepared paste. Fry for a further 2 minutes, then add the beef to the dish.

4. Stir well and cover with the stock and coconut milk. Cook until simmering, then transfer the contents of the dish to a slow cooker, tucking in the lime leaves as well.

5. Cover with a lid and cook on a low setting for 6 hours until the beef is very tender.

6. Remove the lid and cook on a high setting for 10–15 minutes until the gravy thickens. Season to taste with salt and pepper.

7. Spoon into serving dishes and garnish with the coriander before serving.

TOP TIP

Use light coconut milk for a diet version of this curry.

73

Beef Pot Roast

SERVES 6

PREPARATION TIME 25 MINUTES

COOKING TIME 3 HOURS 15 MINUTES

INGREDIENTS

75 ml / 3 fl. oz / ⅓ cup olive oil
1 kg / 2 lb 4 oz beef topside, trimmed and tied
4 cloves of garlic, crushed
4 large carrots, peeled and cut into batons
4 large parsnips, peeled and cut into batons
300 g / 10 ½ oz / 2 cups baby turnips, peeled
250 ml / 9 fl. oz / 1 cup dry white wine
250 ml / 9 fl. oz / 1 cup beef stock
a small bunch of rosemary
2 tbsp flat-leaf parsley, finely chopped
salt and freshly ground black pepper

METHOD

1. Preheat the oven to 150°C (130°C fan) / 300F / gas 2.

2. Heat 2 tbsp of oil in a large casserole dish set over a moderate heat until hot.

3. Season the beef with salt and pepper, then seal in the hot oil until golden all over.

4. Remove from the dish and add a little more of the oil, followed by the garlic and vegetables. Fry for 4–5 minutes, stirring occasionally, until starting to brown.

5. Deglaze the dish with the white wine, then let it reduce by half. Add the stock, stir well and position the beef over the vegetables.

6. Transfer to the oven to roast for 2 hours 30–45 minutes until the beef is tender and registers at least 65°C / 150F on a meat thermometer.

7. Remove from the oven, cover loosely with kitchen foil and leave to rest for at least 15 minutes.

8. Garnish with the herbs before serving.

TOP TIP
Rotate the beef and flip it halfway through roasting.

Chilli Con Carne

SERVES 4

PREPARATION TIME **15 MINUTES**

COOKING TIME **8 HOURS 15 MINUTES**

INGREDIENTS

tbsp sunflower oil

large onion, finely chopped

cloves of garlic, minced

00 g / 1 lb 5 oz / 4 cups beef mince, 20% fat

tsp ground cumin

tsp paprika

pinch of cayenne pepper

00 g / 14 oz / 2 cups canned kidney
    beans, drained

00 g / 14 oz / 2 cups canned chopped tomatoes

00 g / 7 oz / 1 cup canned sweetcorn, drained

50 ml / 1 pint 6 fl. oz / 3 cups beef stock

tbsp jalapeños in vinegar, sliced

our tortillas, to serve

alt and freshly ground black pepper

METHOD

1. Heat the oil in a casserole dish set over
   a medium heat until hot. Add the onion,
   garlic and a pinch of salt.

2. Fry for 4 minutes, stir occasionally, then
   add the mince and brown well all over.

3. Add the spices, stir well and cook for a
   further minute. Stir in the beans, tomatoes,
   sweetcorn and stock.

4. Pour into a slow cooker and cover with a lid.
   Cook on low for 8 hours.

5. Adjust the seasoning to taste and ladle into
   bowls. Garnish with sliced jalapeños and
   serve with tortillas.

TOP TIP

Use extra-lean beef
mince for a diet version.

Korean Beef

SERVES 4

PREPARATION TIME 20 MINUTES

COOKING TIME 3 HOURS 15 MINUTES

INGREDIENTS

600 g / 1 lb 5 oz / 4 cups sirloin steak, cut into
    thin strips
3 tbsp dark soy sauce
1 tbsp fish sauce
3 tbsp sesame oil
450 g / 1 lb / 4 cups green (string)
    beans, trimmed
5 cm (2 in) piece of root ginger, peeled
    and minced
1 red chilli (chili), cut into strips
1 stalk of lemon grass
350 ml / 12 fl. oz / 1 ½ cups beef stock
2 aubergines (eggplants), peeled and diced
a small bunch of coriander (cilantro), chopped
1 lime
salt and freshly ground black pepper

METHOD

1. Marinate the meat with soy sauce and
   fish sauce.

2. Heat the sesame oil in a wok or frying
   pan and gently cook the beans, ginger,
   chilli and lemon grass.

3. Add the stock, aubergine and steak with
   its marinade. Stir well and pour into a
   slow cooker.

4. Cover with a lid and cook on high for
   3 hours until the beef is tender.

5. Stir through the coriander and season
   to taste.

6. Serve on plates and grate over some
   lime zest before serving.

TOP TIP
The beef can be left to marinate for up to 30 minutes before using.

Slow-cooked Steak Pie

SERVES 4

PREPARATION TIME 20 MINUTES

COOKING TIME 5 HOURS

INGREDIENTS

bsp plain (all-purpose) flour

0 g / 2 lb / 6 cups stewing steak, trimmed
and cubed

ml / 2 fl. oz / ¼ cup sunflower oil

arge onion, chopped

nedium carrots, peeled and sliced

0 g / 5 oz / 2 cups closed-cup mushrooms,
quartered

0 ml / 18 fl. oz / 2 cups ale

0 ml / 18 fl. oz / 2 cups beef stock

heets of filo pastry, kept under a damp cloth

bsp butter, melted

g / 2 oz / 1 cup rocket (arugula)

t and freshly ground black pepper

METHOD

1. Sprinkle the flour over the beef and season
   with salt and pepper. Heat 2 tbsp of the oil in
   a large casserole dish set over a moderate
   heat until hot.

2. Seal the beef in batches, using a little fresh
   oil for each, until golden all over. Remove
   from the dish and add the onion, carrots
   and mushrooms.

3. Fry for 5 minutes, stirring frequently, then
   deglaze with the ale. Return the beef to the
   dish and add the stock.

4. Pour into a slow cooker, cover with a lid and
   cook on low for 4 hours.

5. Preheat the oven to 180°C (160°C fan) / 350F
   / gas 4.

6. Season the beef stew with salt and pepper
   before dividing between individual pie dishes.
   Top with the filo pastry sheets, tucking and
   folding them to fit inside the dishes.

7. Brush the pastry with melted butter and
   arrange the dishes on a baking tray. Bake
   for 40–45 minutes until the pastry is golden.

8. Remove from the oven and leave to stand
   briefly before serving with rocket leaves.

TOP TIP

Try substituting the
ale for red wine for a
different taste.

Slow-roasted Pork with Apples

SERVES 4

PREPARATION TIME 20 MINUTES

COOKING TIME 2 HOURS 20 MINUTES

INGREDIENTS

2 x 450 g / 1 lb pork loin racks, French trimmed
2 tbsp sunflower oil
4 small red onions, chopped
2 large Golden Delicious apples, cored and diced
3 sprigs of rosemary, chopped
500 ml / 18 fl. oz / 2 cups ham stock
flaked sea salt and freshly ground black pepper

METHOD

1. Preheat the oven to 220°C (200°C fan) / 425F / gas 7.

2. Rub the pork with sunflower oil and season with plenty of salt and pepper.

3. Arrange half of the onions and apples in a roasting tray. Sit the pork racks on the onions and apples and top with the remaining onion and apples.

4. Sprinkle over the rosemary and pour the stock around the tray but not over the pork.

5. Roast for 20 minutes and then reduce the temperature to 150°C (130°C fan) / 300F / gas 2, cooking for a further 2 hours until the pork is very tender.

6. Remove from the oven and rest, covered loosely, for 10 minutes before serving.

TOP TIP

Ask your butcher to French-trim the pork before using.

Pork Chops

SERVES 4

PREPARATION TIME 20 MINUTES

COOKING TIME 4 HOURS 15 MINUTES

INGREDIENTS

tbsp sunflower oil
centre-cut pork chops, trimmed
large onion, chopped
medium carrots, peeled and diced
sticks of celery, peeled and diced
cloves of garlic, chopped
00 g / 14 oz / 2 cups canned chopped tomatoes
tbsp tomato purée
50 ml / 1 pint 6 fl. oz / 3 cups ham stock
bouquet garni
-5 sprigs of thyme
alt and freshly ground black pepper

METHOD

1. Heat the oil in a casserole dish set over a moderate heat until hot. Season the pork chops and seal in the oil until golden.

2. Reduce the heat a little and add the onion, carrot, celery, garlic, chopped tomatoes, purée and stock, stirring well.

3. Tuck the bouquet garni into the dish and continue to cook until the broth is simmering. Pour everything into a slow cooker, cover with a lid and cook on a low setting for 4 hours.

4. Once the pork is cooked, season the dish with salt and pepper. Serve with a garnish of thyme.

TOP TIP

Let the pork chops stand for 5–10 minutes once cooked before serving.

Stuffed Pork Loin

SERVES 6

PREPARATION TIME 15 MINUTES

COOKING TIME 2 HOURS 10 MINUTES

INGREDIENTS

2 tbsp butter
1 leek, sliced, washed, and drained
300 g / 10 ½ oz / 2 cups dried apricots,
   roughly chopped
a small bunch of thyme
1.25 kg / 2 lb 12 oz pork loin, trimmed
   and butterflied
2 tbsp olive oil
2 onions, chopped
4 sticks of celery, sliced
4 carrots, peeled and sliced
500 ml / 18 fl. oz / 2 cups ham stock
salt and freshly ground pepper

METHOD

1. Preheat the oven to 200°C (180°C fan)
   / 400F / gas 6.

2. Melt the butter in a large frying pan set
   over a medium heat until hot. Add the leek
   and sweat for 5 minutes with a pinch of salt
   until softened.

3. Add the apricots and a few leaves from the
   thyme, then continue to cook for another
   5 minutes. Season to taste.

4. Open the pork up so that it lies flat on
   a chopping board. Season with salt and
   pepper and spoon the leeks and apricot
   down the centre.

5. Roll the sides over and around the filling,
   tying securely at intervals with kitchen string.

6. Rub the outside with olive oil and season
   with salt and pepper. Arrange the onions,
   celery and carrot in a roasting tray.

7. Sit the pork on top and pour the stock
   around it. Roast for 15 minutes, then reduce
   the heat to 150°C (130°C fan) / 300F / gas 2.

8. Roast for a further 1 hour 20–30 minutes
   until the pork is cooked through and
   registers at least 65°C / 149F.

9. Remove from the oven and rest, covered
   loosely with kitchen foil, for 10 minutes
   before slicing and serving with a garnish
   of thyme.

TOP TIP

Roast the pork for an
additional 15–20
minutes for well-
done meat.

Slow-roasted Belly Pork

SERVES 4

PREPARATION TIME **15 MINUTES**

COOKING TIME **3 HOURS**

INGREDIENTS

- 900 g / 2 lb piece of pork belly, trimmed with excess fat removed
- 1 tbsp honey
- 1 tbsp cumin seeds
- 1 tbsp fennel seeds
- 1 tsp coriander seeds
- 1 tbsp olive oil
- 1 tbsp balsamic vinegar
- Few sprigs of bay leaves
- Salt and freshly ground black pepper

METHOD

1. Preheat the oven to 200°C (180°C fan) / 400F / gas 6.

2. Sit the pork belly on a roasting tray and brush with the honey. Lightly crush the cumin, fennel and coriander seeds.

3. Sprinkle over the pork, then drizzle over the oil and balsamic vinegar. Tuck the bay leaves in and around the pork.

4. Roast in the oven for 20 minutes, then reduce the heat to 150°C (130°C fan) / 300F / gas 2.

5. Continue to cook for a further 2 hours 30–40 minutes until the pork is tender.

6. Remove from the oven and rest, covered loosely, for 10 minutes before serving.

TOP TIP

Pour off any rendered fat from the pork belly halfway through roasting.

Pulled Pork Burgers

SERVES 4

PREPARATION TIME 20 MINUTES

COOKING TIME 8 HOURS 20 MINUTES

INGREDIENTS

2 tbsp sunflower oil
3 cloves of garlic, minced
1 onion, finely chopped
1 tsp ground cumin
a pinch of ground cinnamon
a pinch of cayenne pepper
100 ml / 3 ½ fl. oz / ½ cup tomato ketchup
100 ml / 3 ½ fl. oz / ½ cup apple cider vinegar
2 tbsp soft dark brown sugar
500 ml / 18 fl. oz / 2 cups chicken stock
900 g / 2 lb piece of pork shoulder, trimmed
    and scored
½ white cabbage, shredded
2 carrots, peeled and finely grated
1 red onion, chopped
100 g / 3 ½ oz / ½ cup mayonnaise
4 white sandwich rolls, split
125 g / 4 ½ oz / ½ cup barbecue sauce
salt and freshly ground black pepper

METHOD

1. Heat the oil in a large casserole dish set over a moderate heat until hot. Add the onion, garlic and some seasoning and sweat until golden.

2. Add the ground spices, stir well and cook for a further minute. Add the ketchup, vinegar, sugar and chicken stock.

3. Cook until simmering, stir occasionally, then add the pork. Pour into a slow cooker and cover with a lid.

4. Cook on a low setting for 7–8 hours until the pork starts to break apart.

5. Remove the pork from the sauce and pat dry. Shred between two forks and stir back into the slow cooker, seasoning with salt and pepper.

6. Stir together the cabbage, carrot, onion and mayonnaise. Season to taste with salt and pepper.

7. Top the bottom halves of the rolls with pulled pork and a little barbecue sauce. Follow with the coleslaw and sit the tops of the buns in place before serving.

TOP TIP

Baste the pork every couple of hours as it slow cooks.

Sweet and Sour Pork

SERVES 4

PREPARATION TIME 20 MINUTES

COOKING TIME 6 HOURS 20 MINUTES

INGREDIENTS

150 ml / 5 fl. oz / ⅔ cup pineapple juice

100 ml / 4 fl. oz / ½ cup water

1 tbsp distilled vinegar

1 tbsp light soy sauce

75 g / 3 oz / ⅓ cup soft light brown sugar

1 tbsp cornflour (cornstarch)

1 tbsp sesame oil

600 g / 1 lb 5 oz / 4 cups pork loin, sliced

2 onions, chopped

3 cm (1 ¼ in) piece of root ginger, peeled
and minced

1 green pepper, diced

1 red pepper, diced

1 yellow pepper, diced

2 cloves of garlic, minced

500 g / 12 oz / 3 cups cooked rice, to serve

salt and freshly ground black pepper

METHOD

1. Combine the pineapple juice, water, vinegar, soy sauce, sugar and cornflour in a saucepan.

2. Whisk well, cooking over a low heat, until smooth. Continue to cook until simmering and thickened. Set to one side.

3. Heat the sesame oil in a large frying pan set over a moderate heat until hot.

4. Add the pork and fry for 2 minutes, tossing occasionally. Add the ginger, vegetables and garlic and stir well.

5. Tip the pork and vegetables into a slow cooker and cover with the sauce. Cover with a lid and cook on a low setting for 5–6 hours until the pork is tender.

6. Adjust the seasoning to taste and serve over bowls of rice.

TOP TIP
For those allergic to sesame oil, replace it with sunflower oil.

Sticky Slow-cooked Pork Ribs

SERVES 4

PREPARATION TIME 15 MINUTES

COOKING TIME 8 HOURS 25 MINUTES

INGREDIENTS

350 g / 12 oz / 1 ½ cups tomato ketchup
150 ml / 5 fl. oz / ⅔ cup apple cider vinegar
110 g / 4 oz / ⅔ cup soft light brown sugar
1 tsp Dijon mustard
1.35 kg / 3 lb pork spare ribs, trimmed
2 tbsp sunflower oil
salt and freshly ground black pepper

METHOD

1. Combine the ketchup, vinegar, sugar, mustard and seasoning in a saucepan and cook over a low heat, stirring, until smooth.

2. Rub the spare ribs with the oil and season generously with salt and pepper. Heat a large frying pan over a moderate heat until hot.

3. Seal the ribs in the pan until golden all over. Remove from the pan and cut to size, placing in a slow cooker.

4. Brush with some of the barbecue sauce. Cover the slow cooker with a lid and cook the ribs on a low setting for 8 hours until they are meltingly soft, basting with sauce every two hours.

5. Remove the lid and cook on a high setting for a further 10 minutes, basting with more barbecue sauce.

6. Slice and serve with any remaining sauce on the side.

TOP TIP

Turn the ribs over every 2 hours when cooking in the slow cooker.

Glazed Ham Joint

SERVES 8

PREPARATION TIME 10 MINUTES

COOKING TIME 3 HOURS 15 MINUTES

INGREDIENTS

- 0 ml / 12 fl. oz / 1 ½ cups cola
- kg / 7 lb 12 oz ham joint, washed and patted dry
- osp cloves
- osp wholegrain mustard
- t and freshly ground black pepper

METHOD

1. Preheat the oven to 180°C (160°C fan) / 350F / gas 4. Reduce the cola in a pan set over a moderate heat until syrupy.

2. Place the ham joint on a trivet sat inside a large casserole dish. Score a diamond pattern on the outside of the ham and stud with cloves.

3. Brush with some of the reduced cola, then brush with the mustard and season with salt and pepper at the same time.

4. Cover the dish with a lid and bake the ham for 1 hour 30 minutes, then remove the lid.

5. Continue to bake for another 1 hour 20–30 minutes, basting with more cola, until the ham registers at least 71°C / 160F on a meat thermometer.

6. Remove from the oven and leave to cool before slicing and serving.

TOP TIP

Rinse the ham in a couple of changes of cold water when preparing.

Sausage Cassoulet

SERVES 4

PREPARATION TIME 20 MINUTES

COOKING TIME 4 HOURS 15 MINUTES

INGREDIENTS

2 tbsp olive oil
1 onion, chopped
2 cloves of garlic, minced
a pinch of fennel seeds
450 g / 1 lb / 3 cups smoked sausage, cubed
4 vine tomatoes, cored and diced
400 g / 14 oz / 2 cups canned chopped tomatoes
4 medium potatoes, peeled and diced
600 ml / 1 pint 2 fl. oz / 2 ½ cups vegetable stock
a small handful of flat-leaf parsley, chopped
2 sprigs of oregano
150 g / 5 oz / ⅔ cup crème fraiche
a pinch of paprika
salt and freshly ground black pepper

METHOD

1. Heat the olive oil in a large casserole dish set over a medium heat until hot.

2. Add the onion, garlic, fennel seeds and sausage. Fry for 5 minutes, stirring occasionally, then add the vine tomatoes, chopped tomatoes, potatoes and stock.

3. Cook until simmering, then spoon into a slow cooker.

4. Cover the cooker with a lid and cook on a high setting for 4 hours, then adjust the seasoning to taste.

5. Serve with a garnish of herbs, dollops of crème fraiche and a pinch of paprika.

TOP TIP

Hot paprika will lend a little heat to the dish when garnishing.

Slow-roasted Leg of Lamb

SERVES 4

PREPARATION TIME 20 MINUTES

COOKING TIME 2 HOURS 45 HOURS

INGREDIENTS

35 kg / 3 lb leg of lamb on the bone, trimmed
tbsp olive oil
few sprigs of rosemary
00 g / 10 ½ oz / 2 cups new potatoes, peeled
50 g / 1 lb / 3 cups baby carrots
50 g / 9 oz / 2 cups green (string)
   beans, trimmed
50 g / 5 oz / 1 ½ cups fresh peas
5 g / 2 oz / ¼ cup butter, cubed
alt and freshly ground black pepper

METHOD

1. Preheat the oven to 200°C (180°C fan) / 400F / gas 6.

2. Rub the lamb with the olive oil and season with plenty of salt and pepper.

3. Place on a roasting tray and place in the oven. Roast for 20 minutes and then reduce the oven to 150°C (130°C fan) / 300F / gas 3.

4. Roast for another 2 hours until the thickest part of the leg registers at least 60°C / 140F on a meat thermometer.

5. Remove the lamb from the oven and leave to rest, covered loosely, for 20 minutes.

6. Cook the potatoes and carrots in a pan of salted, boiling water for 15 minutes, then add the beans and peas and cook for a further 3 minutes.

7. Drain the vegetables and toss with the butter and seasoning. Serve alongside the lamb.

TOP TIP

Bone-in lamb shoulder makes an alternative cut to the leg.

Braised Lamb Chops

SERVES 4

PREPARATION TIME 15 MINUTES

COOKING TIME 6 HOURS 20 MINUTES

INGREDIENTS

2 tbsp olive oil
4 large lamb chops on the bone, trimmed
4 shallots, halved
400 g / 14 oz / 2 cups canned chickpeas (garbanzo beans), drained
400 g / 14 oz / 2 cups canned kidney beans, drained
750 ml / 1 pint 6 fl. oz / 3 cups vegetable stock
110 ml / 4 fl. oz / ½ cup red wine vinegar
2–3 sprigs of thyme
2–3 sprigs of oregano
salt and freshly ground black pepper

METHOD

1. Drizzle the olive oil over the lamb chops and season with salt and pepper.

2. Heat a large frying pan over a moderate heat until hot. Seal the chops in the pan until golden on both sides.

3. Remove from the pan and set to one side. Add the shallots to the pan and fry over a high heat until lightly charred.

4. Transfer the shallots to a slow cooker. Add the chickpeas, kidney beans, stock and vinegar. Position the chops on top and cover with a lid.

5. Cook on a low setting for 6 hours until the beans are tender and the lamb chops are cooked through.

6. Adjust the seasoning to taste and serve in bowls with a garnish of herbs.

TOP TIP
Substitute the vinegar for red wine for a less acidic sauce.

Stuffed Roast Lamb

SERVES 8

PREPARATION TIME 25 MINUTES

COOKING TIME 2 HOURS 20 MINUTES

INGREDIENTS

- 340 g / 12 oz / 3 cups feta, crumbled
- small bunch of mint, chopped
- small bunch of rosemary, chopped
- 1.5 kg / 3 lb 5 oz leg of lamb, trimmed and butterflied
- 55 ml / 2 fl. oz / ¼ cup olive oil
- head of garlic, cloves separated and sliced
- 225 ml / 8 fl. oz / 1 cup dry white wine
- sea salt and freshly ground black pepper

METHOD

1. Preheat the oven to 170°C (150°C fan) / 325F / gas 3.

2. Combine the feta with the chopped mint, half of the rosemary and some seasoning.

3. Open up the butterflied lamb and spoon the feta down the middle. Bring the lamb up and around the feta filling and tie securely with kitchen string at intervals.

4. Sit in a roasting tray and rub with the olive oil, remaining rosemary and sliced garlic. Season with salt and pepper.

5. Pour the wine into the dish and cover the tray loosely with kitchen foil.

6. Roast for 1 hour. Remove the foil and roast for a further 1 hour 10–20 minutes until the lamb registers at least 63°C / 145F on a meat thermometer.

7. Remove from the oven, cover loosely with kitchen foil and leave to rest for at least 20 minutes before slicing and serving.

TOP TIP

Roast for an extra 20 minutes for well-done meat.

Lamb Tagine

SERVES 4

PREPARATION TIME 20 MINUTES

COOKING TIME 7 HOURS 20 MINUTES

INGREDIENTS

55 ml / 2 fl. oz / ¼ cup olive oil
850 g / 1 lb 14 oz / 5 ⅔ cups lamb shoulder, diced
1 onion, finely chopped
2 cloves of garlic, minced
2 tsp ras el hanout
1 tsp ground cumin
½ tsp paprika
½ tsp ground cinnamon
300 g / 10 ½ oz / 2 cups pitted dates
200 g / 7 oz / 1 cup passata
1 tbsp honey
500 ml / 18 fl. oz / 2 cups lamb stock
400 g / 14 oz / 3 cups cooked couscous
a small handful of flat-leaf parsley, chopped
salt and freshly ground black pepper

METHOD

1. Heat the olive oil in a casserole dish set over a moderate heat until hot.

2. Season the lamb and seal in batches until golden all over. Remove from the dish and reduce the heat slightly.

3. Add the onion, garlic and a little salt and fry for 4 minutes, stirring frequently, then add the ground spices.

4. Return the lamb to the dish and stir in the dates, passata, honey and lamb stock.

5. Pour into a slow cooker, cover with a lid and cook on a low setting for 6–7 hours until the lamb is tender.

6. Season to taste with salt and pepper. Serve over couscous with a garnish of chopped parsley.

TOP TIP

Remember to stir the lamb from time to time as it cooks.

Irish Stew

METHOD

1. Heat the butter and oil in a large casserole dish set over a moderate heat until hot.

2. Sprinkle the flour over the lamb and season with salt and pepper. Seal in the dish, in batches, until golden.

3. Reduce the heat slightly and stir in the vegetables. Cover with the ale and stock, then cook until simmering.

4. Pour into a slow cooker. Cover with a lid and cook on a low setting for 6 hours until the lamb and vegetables are tender.

5. Steam the broccoli in a steaming basket set over a half-filled saucepan of simmering water. Cook for 5–6 minutes until tender.

6. Season the stew with salt and pepper, serving with the steamed broccoli on the side.

SERVES 4

PREPARATION TIME 20 MINUTES

COOKING TIME 6 HOURS 20 MINUTES

INGREDIENTS

tbsp butter
tbsp vegetable oil
tbsp plain (all-purpose) flour
0 g / 2 lb / 6 cups diced lamb
ticks of celery, sliced
arge carrots, peeled and finely diced
0 g / 1 lb / 3 cups turnips, peeled and cubed
0 g / 1 lb / 3 cups floury potatoes, peeled and cubed
0 ml / 9 fl. oz / 1 cup ale
0 ml / 1 pint 6 fl. oz / 3 cups beef stock
arge head of broccoli, prepared into florets
lt and freshly ground black pepper

TOP TIP

A full-bodied ale will give this stew the best taste.

Slow-braised Shepherd's Pie

SERVES 4

PREPARATION TIME 20 MINUTES

COOKING TIME 5 HOURS

INGREDIENTS

2 tbsp sunflower oil
2 onions, finely chopped
4 carrots, diced
600 g / 1 lb 5 oz / 4 cups lamb mince
400 g / 14 oz / 2 cups canned tomatoes, chopped
250 ml / 9 fl. oz / 1 cup beef stock
1 tbsp Worcestershire sauce
850 g / 1 lb 14 oz / 5 ²/₃ cups floury potatoes,
   peeled and diced
2 tbsp butter
110 ml / 4 fl. oz / ½ cup milk
salt and freshly ground black pepper

METHOD

1. Heat the oil in a large saucepan and fry the onion until softened. Add the carrots, cook for 5 minutes and then stir in the lamb, browning well.

2. Add the tomatoes, stock and Worcestershire sauce. Stir, then spoon into a slow cooker.

3. Cover and cook on a low setting for 4 hours. Cook the potatoes in a saucepan of salted, boiling water for 18–22 minutes until tender.

4. Drain well and mash with the butter and milk, seasoning to taste. Cover and set to one side.

5. Once the lamb is ready, season to taste with salt and pepper.

6. Preheat the oven to 180°C (160°C fan) / 350F / gas 4. Divide the lamb between four small baking dishes.

7. Top with the mashed potato and spread it over the lamb with the tines of a fork.

8. Place on a baking tray and bake for around 40–45 minutes until the potato is turning golden brown.

9. Remove from the oven and leave to stand briefly before serving.

TOP TIP
Try using beef mince for a cottage pie.

Lamb Biryani

RVES 4

EPARATION TIME 20 MINUTES

OKING TIME 6 HOURS 20 MINUTES

GREDIENTS

ml / 2 fl. oz / ¼ cup sunflower oil

loves of garlic, finely chopped

m (2 in) piece of root ginger, peeled
and chopped

mall bunch of coriander (cilantro), chopped

arge onion, finely sliced

0 g / 1 lb 10 oz / 5 cups lamb shoulder, diced

sp ground cardamom

sp ground cinnamon

sp ground cloves

sp ground cumin

0 g / 9 oz / 1 ½ cups basmati rice,
rinsed thoroughly

0 ml / 18 fl. oz / 2 cups lamb stock

arge vine tomatoes, peeled and diced

0 g / 5 oz / ⅔ cup Greek yogurt

t and freshly ground black pepper

METHOD

1. Blitz together half the oil with the garlic,
   ginger, coriander and a little salt in a food
   processor until smooth.

2. Heat the remaining oil in a large casserole
   dish set over a moderate heat. Fry the paste
   and onions in the oil for 3 minutes, stirring
   frequently.

3. Add the lamb shoulder and continue to
   cook for 5 minutes. Sprinkle over the ground
   spices, stir well and cook for a further minute.

4. Stir in the rice, cover with the stock and
   cook until simmering. Stir in the tomatoes,
   then transfer the contents of the dish into
   a slow cooker.

5. Cover with a lid and cook on a low setting for
   6 hours until the lamb is tender and the rice
   is cooked.

6. Season to taste with salt and pepper, then
   spoon into bowls and garnish with dollops
   of Greek yogurt.

TOP TIP

When the lamb can be
pulled apart between
your fingers, it
is ready.

Lamb Shanks

SERVES 4

PREPARATION TIME 20 MINUTES

COOKING TIME 8 HOURS 15 MINUTES

INGREDIENTS

55 ml / 2 fl. oz / ¼ cup vegetable oil
4 lamb shanks, trimmed
8 shallots, cut into wedges
4 carrots, sliced
2 cloves of garlic, sliced
2 tsp hot paprika
500 ml / 18 fl. oz / 2 cups lamb stock
110 ml / 4 fl. oz / ½ cup dry sherry
100 g / 3 ½ oz / ⅔ cup sultanas
5 cm (2 in) cinnamon stick
a pinch of chilli (chili) flakes
2 tbsp pistachios, shelled
salt and freshly ground black pepper

METHOD

1. Heat the oil in a casserole dish set over a moderate heat until hot. Season the shank with salt and pepper and seal in the hot oil until golden all over.

2. Transfer to a slow cooker, then add the vegetables, paprika, stock, sherry, sultan cinnamon and a pinch of chilli flakes.

3. Cover with a lid and cook on low for 8 hour until the meat is coming away from the bo

4. Season to taste with salt and pepper and serve with a garnish of chopped pistachios

TOP TIP

Turn over the lamb shanks every 2 hours in the slow cooker.

Fish and Seafood

Whole Baked Salmon

SERVES 4

PREPARATION TIME 20 MINUTES

COOKING TIME 2 HOURS

INGREDIENTS

75 ml / 3 fl. oz / ⅓ cup olive oil
300 g / 10 ½ oz / 6 cups baby spinach, washed
4 cloves of garlic, minced
4 kg / 8 lb 12 oz salmon, gutted and scaled
1 red onion, sliced
250 ml / 9 fl. oz / 1 cup dry white wine
1 lemon, sliced
a small bunch of thyme
salt and freshly ground black pepper

METHOD

1. Preheat the oven to 170°C (150°C fan) / 325F / gas 3.

2. Heat 3 tbsp of oil in a large frying pan and fry the spinach with the garlic, in batches, until wilted. Tip the wilted spinach into a colander and press against the side to extract some of the water.

3. Stuff the gutted salmon with the spinach and red onion. Season with salt and pepper and drizzle with the remaining olive oil.

4. Tie the salmon with kitchen string and lift into a baking dish or roasting tray. Pour in the white wine and top the salmon with lemon slices and more seasoning.

5. Cover the dish with kitchen foil and bake for 1 hour 30–45 minutes until the fish is firm and flakes easily with a fork.

6. Remove from the oven and garnish with thyme before serving.

TOP TIP

Check for any large bones in the salmon before preparing.

Poached Salmon Fillets

SERVES 4

PREPARATION TIME 20–25 MINUTES

COOKING TIME 5 HOURS 25 MINUTES

INGREDIENTS

lemon

peppercorns

skinless salmon fillets

00 g / 1 lb 5 oz / 4 cups Desiree potatoes, peeled

small onions, chopped

small bunch of flat-leaf parsley, finely chopped

tbsp sunflower oil

tbsp unsalted butter

50 g / 9 oz / 1 ²⁄₃ cups cherry tomatoes, halved

large handful of coriander (cilantro),
    finely chopped

red chilli (chili), seeded and diced

ripe avocados, pitted and diced

small onion, chopped

dashes hot sauce

cloves of garlic, finely chopped

5 ml / 2 fl. oz / ¼ cup extra-virgin olive oil

alt and freshly ground black pepper

METHOD

1. Cut a thick slice from the lemon. Heat a shallow pan of water to a simmer, then add the lemon slice, peppercorns and a pinch of salt. Cook for 2 minutes, then pour into a slow cooker.

2. Add the salmon fillets to the slow cooker. Cover and cook on low for 4–5 hours until the salmon is cooked through.

3. Meanwhile, roughly grate the potatoes and dry well using a clean tea towel. Once dried, place in a bowl and add one chopped onion, the parsley and seasoning.

4. Heat together half the oil and butter in a large frying pan set over a medium heat. Drop generous tablespoons of the mixture into the pan, in mounds and spaced apart.

5. Gently flatten the mounds using a spatula or fish slice. Cook for 5–7 minutes until browned underneath.

6. Flip the röstis and cook the other side for 3–4 minutes until lightly browned.

7. Toss together the cherry tomatoes, coriander, chilli, avocado, remaining onion, hot sauce, garlic and olive oil in a mixing bowl.

8. Squeeze in the juice from the remaining lemon and season to taste with salt and pepper. Serve the salmon over the rösti with the avocado and cherry tomato salad spooned over.

TOP TIP

Lightly crush the peppercorns and then add to the water.

Fish Curry

METHOD

1. Heat the sunflower oil in a casserole dish set over a moderate heat until hot.

2. Add the mustard, cumin and coriander seeds. Let them fry and pop for 30 seconds then add the curry powder.

3. Stir well and add the onions, peppers and a pinch of salt, then fry for 3–4 minutes. Add the potatoes, cod, passata and stock.

4. Pour into a slow cooker, cover with a lid and cook on a low setting for 6 hours.

5. Season to taste with salt, pepper and lemon juice, then serve immediately with a garnish of chopped coriander.

SERVES 4

PREPARATION TIME 20 MINUTES

COOKING TIME 6 HOURS 15 MINUTES

INGREDIENTS

55 ml / 2 fl. oz / ¼ cup sunflower oil
1 tsp mustard seeds
1 tsp cumin seeds
½ tsp coriander seeds, crushed
2 tsp mild curry powder
2 large onions, finely sliced
4 red peppers, sliced
4 floury potatoes, peeled and diced
750 g / 1 lb 10 oz / 5 cups skinless cod fillet, diced
200 g / 7 oz / 1 cup passata
750 ml / 1 pint 6 fl. oz / 3 cups fish stock
½ lemon, juiced
a small handful of coriander (cilantro), chopped
salt and freshly ground black pepper

TOP TIP

Desiree or Maris Piper potatoes are perfect in this recipe.

Baked Sea Bass

SERVES 4

PREPARATION TIME **20 MINUTES**

COOKING TIME **5–6 HOURS**

INGREDIENTS

2 fennel bulbs, sliced
1 lemon, juiced
55 ml / 2 fl. oz / ¼ cup olive oil
4 sea bass, gutted and cleaned
400 g / 14 oz / 2 cups canned butter
   beans, drained
200 g / 7 oz / 1 cup passata
1 tsp harissa paste
250 ml / 9 fl. oz / 1 cup fish stock
55 g / 2 oz / 1 cup lamb's lettuce
salt and freshly ground black pepper

METHOD

1. Toss together the fennel, lemon juice,
   olive oil and plenty of seasoning.

2. Stuff the main cavities of the sea bass
   with the fennel and set them aside.

3. Toss together the butter beans, passata,
   harissa and some seasoning. Spoon into
   a slow cooker and cover with the stock.

4. Sit the stuffed sea bass on top of the
   beans and cover the cooker with a lid.

5. Cook on a low setting for 5–6 hours until
   the fish are cooked through and the beans
   are tender.

6. Serve the sea bass and beans with lamb's
   lettuce, seasoned to taste.

TOP TIP
The fish will feel firm yet slightly springy to the touch when ready.

Braised Halibut

SERVES 4

PREPARATION TIME 20 MINUTES

COOKING TIME 6 HOURS

INGREDIENTS

2 large courgettes (zucchinis), diced
2 tbsp olive oil
150 g / 5 oz / 1 cup pitted green olives, sliced
100 g / 3 ½ oz / ⅔ cup sun-dried tomatoes,
    soaked in hot water
2 x 275 g / 10 oz skinless halibut fillets, pin-boned
110 g / 4 oz / ½ cup basil pesto
350 ml / 12 fl. oz / 1 ½ cups vegetable stock
a small handful of curly parsley, roughly chopped
salt and freshly ground black pepper

METHOD

1. Toss the courgette with the olive oil, olives, sun-dried tomato and seasoning.

2. Spoon into a slow cooker and top with the halibut fillets. Spoon over the basil pesto and pour over the vegetable stock.

3. Cover with a lid and cook on a low setting for 6 hours.

4. Season to taste with salt and pepper and serve with a garnish of parsley.

TOP TIP
Baste the halibut from time to time with the stock.

Seafood Paella

INGREDIENTS

- ml / 2 fl. oz / ¼ cup olive oil
- large onion, chopped
- cloves of garlic, minced
- 25 g / 8 oz / 1 ½ cups chorizo, peeled and diced
- 0 g / 10 ½ oz / 1 ½ cups paella rice
- pinch of saffron threads
- 25 l / 2 pints 4 fl. oz / 5 cups chicken stock
- tsp smoked paprika
- vine tomatoes, cored and diced
- 50 g / 1 lb / 3 cups prawns (shrimps), peeled and deveined
- 00 g / 10 ½ oz / 2 cups mussels, cleaned with beards removed
- lemon, juiced
- small handful of flat-leaf parsley, finely chopped
- alt and freshly ground black pepper

METHOD

1. Heat the olive oil in a large, shallow pan and cook the onion, garlic and a pinch of salt for 5 minutes until soft.

2. Add the chorizo and cook for a further 5 minutes, stirring occasionally. Stir in the paella rice and coat thoroughly in the oil.

3. Stir the saffron into the stock, then pour the infused stock over the rice.

4. Add the paprika and stir well, then pour everything into a slow cooker. Cover with a lid and cook on high for 3 hours until the rice is tender.

5. Add the tomatoes, prawns and mussels and cook for a further hour.

6. Stir through the lemon juice and parsley and season to taste before serving.

TOP TIP
If saffron is unavailable, add a pinch of turmeric to the stock, whisking well.

Smoked Haddock Pie

SERVES 4

PREPARATION TIME 20–25 MINUTES

COOKING TIME 7 HOURS 20 MINUTES

INGREDIENTS

110 g / 4 oz / ½ cup butter

150 g / 5 oz / 1 cup pancetta lardons

2 onions, finely sliced

2 tbsp plain (all-purpose) flour

750 ml / 1 pint 6 fl. oz / 3 cups whole milk

750 g / 1 lb 10 oz / 5 cups smoked haddock, diced

1 sprig of thyme, leaves stripped

1 tbsp baby capers in brine, drained

150 ml / 5 fl. oz / ⅔ cup double (heavy) cream

1 kg / 2 lb 4 oz / 6 ⅔ cups Maris Piper potatoes, peeled and grated

salt and freshly ground black pepper

METHOD

1. Melt 2 tbsp of butter in a casserole dish set over a medium heat until hot.

2. Add the pancetta and onions, sweating for 5 minutes until the onion is soft. Remove from the dish.

3. Add another 2 tbsp of butter to the dish, leave to melt, then whisk in the flour. Cook for 1 minute, then whisk in the milk in a slow, steady stream until thickened.

4. Return the onion and bacon, stir in the haddock, thyme leaves and capers, then pour everything into a slow cooker.

5. Cover with a lid and cook on a low setting for 6 hours.

6. Preheat the oven to 180°C (160°C fan) / 350F / gas 4. Season the cod and sauce with salt and pepper and stir in the cream. Pour into a rectangular baking dish.

7. Top with the grated potato and dot with the remaining butter on top. Season with salt and pepper, then bake for 50–60 minutes until the potato is golden and crisp.

8. Leave the pie to stand for 5 minutes before serving.

TOP TIP

Dry the grated potato well before topping the pie with it.

Garlic Mussels

SERVES 4

PREPARATION TIME 15 MINUTES

COOKING TIME 4 HOURS 10 MINUTES

INGREDIENTS

50 ml / 2 fl. oz / ¼ cup olive oil

4 cloves of garlic, chopped

2 shallots, finely chopped

175 ml / 6 fl. oz / ¾ cup dry white wine

900 g / 2 lb / 6 cups mussels, cleaned with beards removed

1 small handful of flat-leaf parsley, chopped

1 small handful of dill, chopped

2 lemons, cut into wedges

Salt and freshly ground black pepper

METHOD

1. Heat the oil in a frying pan set over a medium heat until hot. Add the garlic, shallot and a pinch of salt.

2. Fry for 5 minutes until softened, then deglaze the pan with the wine and pour everything into a slow cooker.

3. Add the mussels and cover the cooker with a lid. Cook on a low setting for 4 hours until the mussels have opened. Discard any that don't.

4. Stir through the chopped herbs and season to taste with salt and pepper. Serve with lemon wedges on the side.

TOP TIP

Try using cider instead of white wine for an apple-tinged broth.

Cod and Vegetable Stew

SERVES 4

PREPARATION TIME 15–20 MINUTES

COOKING TIME 6 HOURS 20 MINUTES

INGREDIENTS

55 ml / 2 fl. oz / ¼ cup olive oil
1 onion, chopped
2 cloves of garlic, crushed
1 red pepper, sliced
1 yellow pepper, sliced
½ small pumpkin, peeled and diced
5 cm (2 in) piece of root ginger, peeled
    and minced
750 ml / 1 pint 6 fl. oz / 3 cups vegetable stock
600 g / 1 lb 5 oz / 4 cups cod fillet, cut into chunks
200 g / 7 oz / 1 cup canned sweetcorn, drained
110 g / 4 oz / 1 cup peas
a few sprigs of thyme, chopped
salt and freshly ground black pepper

METHOD

1. Combine the oil, onion, garlic, peppers, pumpkin, ginger, stock and seasoning in a slow cooker.

2. Cover the cooker with a lid and cook on low for 6 hours until the vegetables are tender.

3. Add the cod, sweetcorn and peas, then cook on high for a further 15–20 minutes until the cod flakes easily.

4. Adjust the seasoning to taste and serve with a garnish of thyme.

TOP TIP

Substitute the vegetable stock for fish for an additional seafood taste.

Cod and Spinach Pasta Bake

SERVES 4

PREPARATION TIME 15 MINUTES

COOKING TIME 5 HOURS

INGREDIENTS

55 g / 2 oz / ¼ cup butter
55 g / 2 oz / ⅓ cup plain (all-purpose) flour
1 l / 1 pint 16 fl. oz / 4 cups whole milk
pinch of nutmeg
450 g / 1 lb / 3 cups skinless cod, diced
350 g / 12 oz / 3 cups penne pasta
110 g / 4 oz / 2 cups baby spinach, washed
100 g / 3 ½ oz / 1 cup golden breadcrumbs
100 g / 3 ½ oz / 1 cup Parmesan, grated
salt and freshly ground black pepper

METHOD

1. Melt the butter in a large saucepan set over a medium heat until hot. Whisk in the flour until a smooth roux forms.

2. Cook for 1 minute, then whisk in the milk in a slow, steady stream until the sauce is completely smooth.

3. Cook for 5 minutes over a reduced heat, until thickened. Season to taste with salt, pepper and nutmeg.

4. Add the cod and pasta and stir, then pour everything into a slow cooker.

5. Cover the cooker with a lid and cook on a low setting for 4 hours.

6. Preheat the oven to 180°C (160°C fan) / 350F / gas 4.

7. Stir the spinach into the fish and pasta. Spoon into a baking dish and top with the breadcrumbs and Parmesan.

8. Bake for 20–25 minutes until golden on top. Leave to stand for 5 minutes before serving.

TOP TIP

Glaze the bake under a hot grill before serving for a crispy, golden finish.

Octopus and Chorizo Stew

SERVES 4

PREPARATION TIME 20 MINUTES

COOKING TIME 6 HOURS 15 MINUTES

INGREDIENTS

2 tbsp olive oil

300 g / 10 ½ oz / 2 cups chorizo, sliced

4 cloves of garlic, minced

1 onion, finely chopped

1 tsp smoked paprika

½ tsp ground cumin

450 g / 1 lb / 3 cups floury potatoes, peeled and
    roughly chopped

400 g / 14 oz / 2 cups passata

1 l / 1 pint 16 fl. oz / 4 cups vegetable stock

450 g / 1 lb / 3 cups octopus tentacles, washed
    and roughly chopped

1 lemon, halved

a small handful of flat-leaf parsley,
    finely chopped

salt and freshly ground black pepper

METHOD

1. Heat the olive oil in a casserole dish set over
   a medium heat until hot. Add the chorizo and
   fry for 2 minutes, then add the garlic, onion
   and a pinch of salt.

2. Fry for 3 minutes, stirring occasionally, then
   stir in the spices. Add the potatoes, passata
   and stock.

3. Stir well and pour into a slow cooker, then
   add the octopus and stir again, covering with
   a lid. Cook on a low setting for 6 hours until
   the octopus is tender.

4. Season to taste with a squeeze of lemon
   juice and some salt and pepper. Garnish with
   chopped parsley and a grating of lemon zest
   before serving.

TOP TIP

If using frozen octopus, leave to thaw completely before using.

Fish Stew

METHOD

1. Heat the olive oil in a casserole dish set over a medium heat until hot.

2. Add the leek, garlic and a little salt. Sweat for 5 minutes, stir occasionally, until softened.

3. Add the paprika and oregano, stir well and cover with the chopped tomatoes and stock.

4. Add the fish, stir well and pour everything into a slow cooker. Cover and cook on low for 5–6 hours until the fish is starting to flake.

5. Season to taste with salt and pepper and garnish with chopped parsley before serving.

ERVES 4

REPARATION TIME 20 MINUTES

OOKING TIME 6 HOURS 15 MINUTES

NGREDIENTS

5 ml / 2 fl. oz / ¼ cup olive oil
leek, sliced and washed
cloves of garlic, minced
tsp paprika
tsp dried oregano
00 g / 14 oz / 2 cups canned chopped tomatoes
l / 1 pint 16 fl. oz / 4 cups fish stock
00 g / 1 lb 5 oz / 4 cups firm, white fish,
   pin-boned and chopped
small handful of flat-leaf parsley, chopped
alt and freshly ground black pepper

TOP TIP

Monkfish or halibut are ideal varieties for this stew.

Vegetable Dishes and Sides

Asparagus and Lemon Risotto

SERVES 4

PREPARATION TIME 15 MINUTES

COOKING TIME 4 HOURS 45 MINUTES

INGREDIENTS

850 ml / 1 pint 9 fl. oz / 3 ½ cups vegetable stock
225 g / 8 oz / 1 ¼ cups Arborio rice
75 ml / 3 fl. oz / ⅓ cup dry white wine
55 ml / 2 fl. oz / ½ cup olive oil
2 cloves of garlic, minced
225 g / 8 oz / 2 cups green asparagus, woody ends
    removed and halved
225 g / 8 oz / 2 cups white asparagus, woody ends
    removed and halved
150 g / 5 oz / 2 cups portobello mushrooms,
    brushed clean and sliced
55 ml / 2 fl. oz / ½ cup double (heavy) cream
100 g / 3 ½ oz / 1 cup Parmesan, grated
1 lemon, halved
salt and freshly ground black pepper

METHOD

1. Combine the stock, rice, wine, oil and garlic in a slow cooker.

2. Cover with a lid and cook on a medium setting for 4 hours until the rice is tender. Stir in the asparagus, mushrooms, cream and Parmesan.

3. Cover and cook for 30–40 minutes until the asparagus is tender. Season to taste with salt and pepper.

4. Halve the lemon and squeeze the juice from half into the risotto. Season again with salt and pepper.

5. Ladle into bowls and grate over some lemon zest before serving.

TOP TIP

Peel any larger asparagus spears so that they are all the same thickness.

Spicy Pumpkin Curry

ERVES 4

REPARATION TIME 20 MINUTES

OOKING TIME 7 HOURS 30 MINUTES

NGREDIENTS

5 ml / 2 fl. oz / ¼ cup vegetable oil
onions, sliced
cloves of garlic, minced
cm (2 in) piece of root ginger, peeled
and minced
tsp ground cumin
tsp ground coriander
2 tsp mild curry powder
2 tsp turmeric
2 tsp caster (superfine) sugar
2 pumpkin, peeled, seeded and diced
00 ml / 18 fl. oz / 2 cups vegetable stock
25 g / 8 oz / 2 cups petit pois
.our tortillas or chapattis, to serve
alt and freshly ground black pepper

METHOD

1. Heat the vegetable oil in a casserole dish set over a medium heat until hot.

2. Add the onion, garlic, ginger and seasoning. Sweat for 5 minutes, stirring frequently.

3. Add the ground spices and sugar, stir well and cook for a further minute.

4. Add the pumpkin and stock. Stir well and pour into a slow cooker.

5. Cover the cooker with a lid and cook on low for 6–7 hours until the pumpkin is tender. Add the peas, stir well and cook on high for a further 20 minutes.

6. Season to taste with salt and pepper, then serve with the tortillas or chapattis on the side.

TOP TIP

Add 1 tsp of chilli (chili) powder for a spicier curry.

Winter Vegetable Stew

SERVES 4

PREPARATION TIME 15–20 MINUTES

COOKING TIME 6 HOURS

INGREDIENTS

2 tbsp olive oil
1 onion, chopped
2 cloves of garlic, chopped
450 g / 1 lb / 3 cups carrots, chopped
2 sticks of celery, chopped
250 g / 9 oz / 2 cups cavolo nero, chopped
400 g / 14 oz / 2 cups canned white
    beans, drained
300 g / 10 ½ oz / 2 cups ripe tomatoes, quartered
200 g / 7 oz / 1 cup passata
1 l / 1 pint 16 fl. oz / 4 cups vegetable stock
100 g / 3 ½ oz / ½ cup basil pesto, to serve
salt and freshly ground black pepper

METHOD

1. Combine the oil and vegetables with the passata and stock in a slow cooker.

2. Cover the cooker with a lid and cook on a low setting for 6 hours, stirring from time to time.

3. Adjust the seasoning to taste and serve with basil pesto on the side.

TOP TIP

Cavolo nero can be substituted with mustard greens or chard.

Slow-cooked Ratatouille

SERVES 4

PREPARATION TIME **15–20 MINUTES**

COOKING TIME **6 HOURS 10 MINUTES**

INGREDIENTS

55 ml / 2 fl. oz / ¼ cup olive oil

1 leek, washed and roughly sliced

2 fennel bulbs, sliced

2 cloves of garlic, minced

2 carrots, peeled and diced

2 red peppers, roughly diced

2 floury potatoes, peeled and diced

1.25 l / 2 pints 4 fl. oz / 5 cups vegetable stock

1 pinch of crushed red pepper flakes

2 tbsp flat-leaf parsley, chopped

2 tbsp dill, chopped

salt and freshly ground black pepper

METHOD

1. Heat the olive oil in a casserole dish set over a medium heat until hot.

2. Add the leek, fennel, garlic and carrot. Sweat with a pinch of salt for 5 minutes, stirring frequently.

3. Add the peppers, potatoes, stock and crushed red pepper flakes. Stir well and pour everything into a slow cooker.

4. Cover with a lid and cook on a low setting for 5–6 hours until the vegetables are tender. Season with salt and pepper.

5. Serve with a garnish of chopped herbs.

TOP TIP

Give the ratatouille a stir from time to time as it cooks.

Chickpea Curry

SERVES 4

PREPARATION TIME 15 MINUTES

COOKING TIME 4 HOURS 15 MINUTES

INGREDIENTS

55 ml / 2 fl. oz / ¼ cup sunflower oil
1 onion, finely chopped
2 cloves of garlic, minced
5 cm (2 in) piece of root ginger, peeled
    and minced
2 tsp ground cumin
2 tsp ground coriander
2 tsp garam masala
1 tsp paprika
a pinch of caster (superfine) sugar
800 g / 1 lb 12 oz / 4 cups canned chickpeas
    (garbanzo beans), drained
200 g / 7 oz / 1 cup canned chopped tomatoes
750 ml / 1 pint 6 fl. oz / 3 cups vegetable stock
a small handful of coriander (cilantro), torn
salt and freshly ground black pepper

METHOD

1. Heat the oil in a large saucepan set over a medium heat until hot.

2. Add the onion, garlic, ginger and a pinch of salt, then fry for 5 minutes, stirring occasionally, until softened.

3. Add the spices and sugar, stir well and continue to cook for a further minute.

4. Stir in the chickpeas, chopped tomatoes and vegetable stock. Pour everything into a slow cooker and cover with a lid.

5. Cook on a high setting for 4 hours until the chickpeas are tender.

6. Adjust the seasoning to taste and serve with a garnish of coriander on top.

TOP TIP

Soak dried chickpeas in water overnight before draining and using.

Vegetarian Enchiladas

SERVES 4

PREPARATION TIME 15 MINUTES

COOKING TIME 4 HOURS 45 MINUTES

INGREDIENTS

60 ml / 2 fl. oz / ¼ cup olive oil

200 g / 7 oz / 1 cup canned sweetcorn, drained

250 g / 9 oz / 2 cups fresh peas

2 sticks of celery, diced

1 onion, finely chopped

1 tsp dried oregano

1 tsp paprika

500 ml / 18 fl. oz / 2 cups vegetable stock

8 flour tortillas

400 g / 14 oz / 2 cups plain yogurt

1 small handful of coriander (cilantro), chopped

150 g / 5 oz / 1 ½ cups Cheddar, grated

½ iceberg lettuce, shredded

4 spring onions (scallions), finely sliced

salt and freshly ground black pepper

METHOD

1. Combine the oil, sweetcorn, peas, celery, onion, herbs, stock and seasoning in a slow cooker.

2. Cover the cooker with a lid and cook on a low setting for 4 hours.

3. Preheat the oven to 180°C (160°C fan) / 350F / gas 4.

4. Fill the tortillas with the vegetable filling and roll to enclose. Mix the yogurt with half of the coriander and some seasoning.

5. Spread over the base of a baking dish and sit the rolled tortillas on top. Sprinkle over the grated cheese and bake for 35–40 minutes until the cheese is melted and golden.

6. Remove from the oven and serve with a garnish of lettuce, spring onion and the remaining coriander.

TOP TIP

Add a handful of sliced chorizo to the filling for a meat version of the enchiladas.

Mushroom Ragout

SERVES 4

PREPARATION TIME 20 MINUTES

COOKING TIME 7 HOURS 20 MINUTES

INGREDIENTS

75 ml / 3 fl. oz / ⅓ cup sunflower oil
1 kg / 2 lb 4 oz venison shoulder, trimmed
and diced
1 tbsp juniper berries
1 tsp white peppercorns
2 cloves
750 ml / 1 pint 6 fl. oz / 3 cups red wine
750 ml / 1 pint 6 fl. oz / 3 cups beef stock
500 g / 18 oz / 3 ⅓ cups small onions, halved,
if necessary
1 tbsp brown sugar
150 g / 5 oz / 1 cup cranberries
400 g / 14 oz / 5 ½ cups mixed wild mushrooms
salt and freshly ground black pepper

METHOD

1. Heat 2 tbsp of oil in a large saucepan set over a moderate heat until hot.

2. Season the venison and seal, in batches, until golden all over, using a little fresh oil for each batch.

3. Reduce the heat a little and add all the remaining ingredients, apart from the mushrooms, then stir well.

4. Tip into a slow cooker, cover with a lid and cook on a low setting for 5 hours.

5. Add the mushrooms, stir and cook for a further 2 hours until the venison is very tender.

6. Season the ragout with salt and pepper before serving.

TOP TIP

Lightly crush the juniper berries to release their full taste.

Parsnip and Carrot Bake

SERVES 4

PREPARATION TIME 20 MINUTES

COOKING TIME 5 HOURS

INGREDIENTS

55 g / 2 oz / ¼ cup butter
large carrots, peeled and cut into batons
large parsnips, peeled and cut into batons
750 ml / 1 pint 6 fl. oz / 3 cups whole milk
75 g / 3 oz / ¾ cup Cheddar, grated
55 g / 2 oz / ½ cup almonds, chopped
55 g / 2 oz / ½ cup walnuts, crushed
tbsp sunflower seeds
salt and freshly ground black pepper

METHOD

1. Melt the butter in a large saucepan set over a medium heat until hot.

2. Add the carrots, parsnips and a pinch of salt. Cook for 5 minutes, stirring occasionally, until slightly softened.

3. Tip into a slow cooker and cover the vegetables with the milk. Cover with a lid and cook on a low setting for 4 hours until tender to the point of a knife.

4. Preheat the oven to 180°C (160°C fan) / 350F / gas 4. Pour the carrots, parsnips and milk into a round baking dish.

5. Top with the cheese, nuts and sunflower seeds and season with salt and pepper.

6. Bake for 40–45 minutes until golden brown on top. Leave to stand for 5 minutes, then serve immediately.

TOP TIP

Grease the dish with a little softened butter to prevent sticking.

Stuffed Tomatoes

SERVES 4

PREPARATION TIME 15 MINUTES

COOKING TIME 3 HOURS 20 MINUTES

INGREDIENTS

4 beef tomatoes
55 ml / 2 fl. oz / ¼ cup olive oil
1 onion, finely chopped
2 cloves of garlic, minced
1 red pepper, finely diced
2 tsp tomato purée
1 tsp paprika
½ tsp dried oregano
300 g / 10 ½ oz / 2 ½ cups cooked long-grain rice
a small bunch of flat-leaf parsley, finely chopped
100 g / 3 ½ oz / 1 cup goats' cheese, crumbled
2 tbsp extra-virgin olive oil
salt and freshly ground black pepper

METHOD

1. Remove the tops from the tomatoes and scoop out the flesh and seeds. Reserve the tops for later.

2. Heat the oil in a casserole dish set over a medium heat until hot, then add the onion, garlic, pepper and a little salt, sweating for 5 minutes until softened.

3. Stir in the tomato purée, paprika and dried oregano. Cook for 1 minute, then stir in the rice, cooking for 3 minutes.

4. Season the rice with salt and pepper, then spoon into the tomatoes and top with goats' cheese and their tops.

5. Position them in a slow cooker, side by side. Cover the slow cooker with a lid and cook on a high setting for 2–3 hours until the tomatoes are tender.

6. Serve with a drizzle of extra-virgin olive oil.

TOP TIP

The flesh and seeds of the tomatoes can be used in the stuffing if desired.

Stuffed Mushrooms

SERVES 4

PREPARATION TIME **15 MINUTES**

COOKING TIME **1 HOUR**

INGREDIENTS

- 150 g / 5 oz / 1 cup sun-dried tomatoes in oil, drained and chopped
- 200 g / 7 oz / 1 ⅓ cups pitted black olives, chopped
- 1 large egg, beaten
- 350 g / 12 oz / 3 cups grated mozzarella
- 1 small bunch of flat-leaf parsley, chopped
- 8 large chestnut mushrooms, brushed clean
- 60 ml / 2 fl. oz / ¼ cup olive oil
- salt and freshly ground black pepper

METHOD

1. Preheat the oven to 170°C (150°C fan) / 325F / gas 3.

2. Stir together the sun-dried tomatoes, olives, egg, mozzarella, parsley and seasoning in a mixing bowl.

3. Remove the stems from the mushrooms and spoon in the mozzarella filling.

4. Arrange the mushrooms in a roasting dish and drizzle with olive oil.

5. Bake for 1 hour until golden brown and tender. Season with a little more black pepper before serving.

TOP TIP
Swap the mozzarella for fresh breadcrumbs to create a dairy-free version.

Baked Onions

SERVES 6

PREPARATION TIME 15 MINUTES

COOKING TIME 4 HOURS 30 MINUTES

INGREDIENTS

3 white onions
3 red onions
2 tbsp olive oil
500 g / 1 lb 2 oz / 3 ⅓ cups pork mince
100 g / 3 ½ oz / 2 cups fresh breadcrumbs
2 cloves of garlic, minced
1 red pepper, chopped
½ tsp dried rosemary
½ tsp dried thyme
800 g / 1 lb 12 oz / 4 cups canned chopped
   tomatoes
100 g / 3 ½ oz / 1 cup Cheddar, grated
6 sprigs of thyme
1 large egg, beaten
salt and freshly ground black pepper

METHOD

1. Peel the onions and remove their tops. Use a paring knife to help cut out and remove the inner layers of the onions.

2. Pulse together the olive oil, pork mince, breadcrumbs, garlic, pepper, dried herbs, egg and seasoning in a food processor until thoroughly mixed.

3. Fill the onions with the mixture, arrange in a slow cooker, then spoon the chopped tomatoes around them and cover the cooker with a lid.

4. Cook on a high setting for 4 hours until the onions are tender, then sprinkle over the cheese and cook, uncovered, for 15 minutes until the cheese has melted.

5. Serve the onions with a garnish of thyme on top.

TOP TIP
Make sure to use fresh, firm onions in this recipe for best results.

Slow-roasted Parsnips

SERVES 4

PREPARATION TIME **15 MINUTES**

COOKING TIME **2 HOURS 5–10 MINUTES**

INGREDIENTS

1 kg / 2 lb 4 oz / 6 ⅔ cups parsnips, peeled and halved

85 g / 3 oz / ⅓ cup honey, warmed

4 sprigs of thyme, leaves stripped

Flaked sea salt and freshly ground black pepper

METHOD

1. Preheat the oven to 150°C (130°C fan) / 300F / gas 2.

2. Toss the parsnips with the honey, thyme and seasoning.

3. Arrange in a roasting dish, cover with kitchen foil and roast for 1 hour 20–30 minutes until tender to the point of a knife.

4. Remove the foil and increase the oven temperature to 190°C (170°C fan) / 375F / gas 5.

5. Roast for a further 25–30 minutes until glazed before serving.

TOP TIP

Other woody herbs such as rosemary work well in this recipe.

Spiced Red Cabbage

SERVES 4

PREPARATION TIME 10–15 MINUTES

COOKING TIME 7 HOURS

INGREDIENTS

1 large red cabbage, shredded
5 cm (2 in) piece of cinnamon
1 tsp cloves
½ tsp cardamom pods
150 g / 5 oz / 1 cup cranberries
500 ml / 18 fl. oz / 2 cups red wine
110 g / 4 oz / ⅔ cup soft light brown sugar
110 ml / 4 fl. oz / ½ cup apple cider vinegar
salt and freshly ground black pepper

METHOD

1. Combine the cabbage, spices, cranberries, red wine, sugar, vinegar and seasoning in a slow cooker.

2. Stir well, cover with a lid and cook on a low setting for 6–7 hours until the cabbage is soft.

3. Adjust the seasoning to taste before serving in bowls.

TOP TIP

Give the cabbage a stir from time to time when it is cooking in the slow cooker.

Slow Baked Beans

SERVES 4

PREPARATION TIME **10 MINUTES**

COOKING TIME **5 HOURS 15 MINUTES**

INGREDIENTS

450 g / 1 lb / 2 ⅔ cups dried haricot beans,
  soaked in water overnight
1 red pepper, diced
400 g / 14 oz / 2 cups canned chopped tomatoes
200 g / 7 oz / 1 cup passata
500 ml / 18 fl. oz / 2 cups vegetable stock
55 g / 2 oz / 1 cup lamb's lettuce
salt and freshly ground black pepper

METHOD

1. Preheat the oven to 150°C (130°C fan) /
   300F / gas 2.

2. Drain the beans and mix with the pepper,
   chopped tomatoes, passata and seasoning
   in a large casserole dish.

3. Cover with the stock and set the dish over
   a medium heat. Cook for 10 minutes, then
   cover with a lid and transfer to the oven.

4. Bake for 4–5 hours, stirring from time to
   time, until the beans are very tender.

5. Adjust the seasoning to taste and serve
   with a garnish of lamb's lettuce.

TOP TIP

Add 1 tsp of smoked
paprika to the beans
for a smoky version.

Potato Dauphinoise

SERVES 4

PREPARATION TIME 20 MINUTES

COOKING TIME 2 HOURS 15 MINUTES

INGREDIENTS

500 ml / 18 fl. oz / 2 cups whole milk

250 ml / 9 fl. oz / 1 cup double (heavy) cream

2 cloves of garlic, crushed

a few sprigs of thyme

1 kg / 2 lb 4 oz / 6 ⅔ cups floury potatoes, peeled and sliced

2 tbsp butter, softened

1 onion, sliced

2 tbsp black poppy seeds

salt and freshly ground black pepper

METHOD

1. Preheat the oven to 150°C (130°C fan) / 300F / gas 2. Warm the milk, cream, garlic and thyme in a saucepan until simmering.

2. Strain into a jug and set to one side. Rinse the potatoes in a bowl of water, then drain and pat dry with kitchen paper.

3. Butter a baking dish and pour in some of the milk and cream. Layer the potato and onion on top and season with salt and pepper in between each layer.

4. Pour over the rest of the milk and cream and cover with foil, then bake for 1 hour 40–45 minutes until tender.

5. Remove the foil and sprinkle over the poppy seeds. Return the dish to the oven for 15–20 minutes to brown on top.

6. Leave to stand for 5 minutes, then serve.

TOP TIP

Season generously and evenly between the layers for best results.

Slow-baked Potatoes

SERVES 4

PREPARATION TIME 15 MINUTES

COOKING TIME 2 HOURS 50 MINUTES

INGREDIENTS

4 large floury potatoes
2 tbsp sunflower oil
150 g / 5 oz / 1 cup pancetta, diced
2 shallots, finely chopped
2 tbsp butter
110 ml / 4 fl. oz / ½ cup whole milk
175 g / 6 oz / 1 ¾ cups Cheddar, grated
2 tbsp flat-leaf parsley, chopped
salt and freshly ground black pepper

METHOD

1. Preheat the oven to 170°C (150°C fan) / 325F / gas 3.

2. Prick the potatoes several times with a fork. Rub with oil and sprinkle with salt. Place on a baking tray and bake for 2 hours 5–15 minutes until tender.

3. Increase the oven to 180°C (160°C fan) / 350F / gas 4.

4. Heat a frying pan over a moderate heat until hot. Add the bacon and fry for 3 minutes, until golden. Add the shallots and cook for a further 2 minutes.

5. Cut the baked potatoes in half and scoop out the insides into a bowl. Mash the potato with the butter and milk, beating until smooth. Stir in the grated cheese, bacon, shallots, parsley and seasoning.

6. Arrange the skins on a baking tray, then spoon the mixture into the potato skins and bake for 20–25 minutes, until the filling is bubbling and golden.

TOP TIP

Russet or King Edward potatoes are ideal for baking.

Puddings and Preserves

Slow Cooker Rice Pudding

SERVES 4

PREPARATION TIME 10 MINUTES

COOKING TIME 2 HOURS 45 MINUTES

INGREDIENTS

150 g / 5 oz / ¾ cup pudding rice
1 tsp lemon zest
750 ml / 1 pint 6 fl. oz / 3 cups whole milk
150 g / 5 oz / ⅔ cup caster (superfine) sugar
1 tsp vanilla pod, seeds scraped out
a pinch of salt
a pinch of ground cinnamon
55 g / 2 oz / ¼ cup unsalted butter, melted
100 ml / 3 ½ fl. oz / ½ cup double (heavy) cream
4 canned peach slices, drained

METHOD

1. Combine the rice, lemon zest, milk, sugar, vanilla pod and seeds, salt and ground cinnamon in a slow cooker. Pour over the melted butter.

2. Cover with a lid and cook on a high setting for 2 hours 30–45 minutes until the rice has absorbed the milk and is tender.

3. Stir through the double cream and spoon into bowls. Serve with a garnish of peach slices on top.

TOP TIP

Arborio or short grain rice work as alternatives to pudding rice.

Ginger Sponge Pudding

SERVES 4

PREPARATION TIME 15 MINUTES

COOKING TIME 3 HOURS 20 MINUTES

INGREDIENTS

110 g / 4 oz / ½ cup margarine, softened

110 g / 4 oz / ½ cup caster (superfine) sugar

2 large eggs

1 tbsp golden syrup

1 tsp ground ginger

a pinch of ground cinnamon

a pinch of salt

110 g / 4 oz / ⅔ cup self-raising flour, sifted

2 tbsp butter, softened

225 g / 8 oz / 1 cup crystallized ginger in syrup

METHOD

1. Cream together the margarine and sugar in a mixing bowl until pale and smooth.

2. Beat in the eggs, one by one, followed by the golden syrup, spices, salt and flour. Beat well until it reaches the consistency of cake batter.

3. Grease a 900 g / 2 lb pudding bowl with the butter. Remove the ginger from the syrup and chop.

4. Spoon half of the ginger and its syrup into the base of the pudding bowl. Top with the batter.

5. Smooth the top and loosely cover the bowl with a sheet of kitchen foil. Sit the pudding bowl in a slow cooker and pour enough boiling water to come halfway up the sides of the bowl.

6. Cover the cooker with a lid and cook the pudding on high for 1 hour. Reduce to low and cook for a further 2 hours 10–20 minutes until a toothpick comes out clean when inserted into the centre of the pudding.

7. Remove to a wire rack to cool before turning out and serving with the rest of the crystallized ginger and syrup spooned over.

TOP TIP

Try using fresh grated ginger instead of ground for an added kick.

Chocolate and Coffee Cheesecake

SERVES *8*

PREPARATION TIME *5 HOURS 20 MINUTES*

COOKING TIME *1 HOUR*

INGREDIENTS

250 g / 9 oz / 1 ⅔ cups digestive biscuits, crushed

150 g / 5 oz / 1 cup unsalted butter, melted

500 g / 1 lb 2 oz / 2 ½ cups cream cheese, softened

110 g / 4 oz / ½ cup caster (superfine) sugar

2 tbsp plain (all-purpose) flour

150 g / 5 oz / 1 cup milk chocolate, chopped

2 tsp instant coffee granules, dissolved in 2 tbsp hot water

2 medium eggs

150 g / 5 oz / 1 cup cherries

METHOD

1. Pulse together the biscuits and melted butter in a food processor. Tip into a 20 cm (8 in) fluted tart tin.

2. Press well into the base and sides of the tin and chill until needed. Preheat the oven to 150°C (130°C fan) / 300F / gas 2.

3. Beat together the cream cheese, sugar and flour in a mixing bowl for 3 minutes until smooth.

4. Melt the chocolate in a heatproof bowl set over a half-filled saucepan of simmering water. Beat into the cream cheese and then beat in the coffee liquid and the eggs, one by one, until smooth.

5. Pour into the biscuit base and sit the tin on a large piece of kitchen foil. Bring the foil up and around the tin and place it in a roasting tray. Pour in enough boiling water to come half way up the sides of the tin.

6. Bake for 1 hour until the cheesecake is set. Remove from the oven and leave it to cool to room temperature.

7. Chill for 4 hours. Turn out, slice and serve with a garnish of cherries.

TOP TIP

Use low-fat cream cheese for a lighter version of this tart.

Blueberry Custard Tart

SERVES *8*

PREPARATION TIME **10 MINUTES**

COOKING TIME **2 HOURS 20 MINUTES**

INGREDIENTS

225 g / 8 oz ready-made shortcrust pastry
a little plain (all-purpose) flour, for dusting
350 g / 12 oz / 3 cups blueberries
600 ml / 1 pint 2 fl. oz / 2 ½ cups water
110 g / 4 oz / ½ cup caster (superfine) sugar
1 tsp vanilla extract
8 medium eggs
250 ml / 9 fl. oz / 1 cup evaporated milk
1 tbsp icing (confectioners') sugar
250 g / 9 oz / 1 cup crème fraiche, to serve

METHOD

1. Preheat the oven to 150°C (130°C fan) / 300F / gas 2.

2. Roll out the pastry on a lightly floured surface into a large round approximately 1 cm (½ in) thick. Use it to line the base and sides of a 20 cm (8 in) fluted tart tin, cutting away any excess pastry.

3. Prick the base with a fork and fill with the blueberries.

4. Combine the water with the sugar and vanilla extract in a saucepan. Cook over a moderate heat, stirring, until the sugar has dissolved.

5. Remove from the heat and leave it to cool. Beat the eggs in a mixing bowl and gently whisk into the syrup along with the evaporated milk.

6. Strain the filling into a jug and pour over the blueberries in the pastry. Bake for 1 hour 30–45 minutes until the pastry is cooked and the filling is set.

7. Increase the oven to 200°C (180°C fan) / 400F / gas 6 and bake for a further 5–10 minutes until golden on top.

8. Remove to a wire rack to cool, then serve with a dusting of icing sugar and crème fraiche on the side.

TOP TIP

Rotate the tart halfway through baking to ensure even cooking of the pastry.

Apple and Blackberry Crumble

SERVES 4

PREPARATION TIME 15 MINUTES

COOKING TIME 2 HOURS 45 MINUTES

INGREDIENTS

2 large Bramley apples, peeled and diced
450 g / 1 lb / 3 cups blackberries
1 tbsp lemon juice
1 tsp ground cinnamon
2 tbsp caster (superfine) sugar
175 g / 6 oz / 1 ¼ cups plain (all-purpose) flour
110 g / 4 oz / ½ cup unsalted butter, cubed
85 g / 3 oz / ½ cup soft light brown sugar
75 g / 3 oz / ½ cup rolled oats

METHOD

1. Combine the apple, blackberries, lemon juice, cinnamon and sugar in a slow cooker.

2. Stir well, cover with a lid and cook on a medium setting for 2 hours.

3. Preheat the oven to 180°C (160°C fan) / 350F / gas 4.

4. Pulse together the flour, butter, sugar and oats in a food processor until the mixture resembles breadcrumbs.

5. Spoon the fruit from the slow cooker into four individual baking dishes and top with the crumble mixture.

6. Bake the crumbles for 40–45 minutes until golden on top. Leave to stand for a few minutes before serving.

TOP TIP

Add more oats to the crumble topping to suit your tastes.

Lemon Cake

SERVES 8

PREPARATION TIME **15 MINUTES**

COOKING TIME **2 HOURS 45 MINUTES**

INGREDIENTS

150 g / 5 oz / ⅔ cup margarine, softened

150 g / 5 oz / ⅔ cup caster (superfine) sugar

150 g / 5 oz / 1 cup self-raising flour

3 large eggs

1 tsp lemon extract

a small handful of candied lemon slices, chopped

1 lemon, juiced

125 g / 4 ½ oz / 1 cup icing (confectioners') sugar

METHOD

1. Beat together the margarine, caster sugar, flour, eggs and lemon extract in a mixing bowl for 3 minutes until pale and smooth.

2. Grease and line a 900 g / 2 lb loaf tin with greaseproof paper, then fold the chopped lemon slices into the batter and spoon into the lined tin.

3. Sit the tin in a slow cooker and cover with kitchen foil. Cover the cooker with a lid. Cook on low for 1 hour, then increase the heat to high and cook for 1 hour 30–45 minutes until golden on top and a cake tester comes out clean from its centre.

4. Remove from the slow cooker and leave to cool on a wire rack.

5. Stir together the lemon juice and icing sugar until smooth and pourable.

6. Once the cake is cool, turn it out from the tin and drizzle its top with the icing before serving.

TOP TIP

This loaf can also be slow-baked in a 130°C / 275F / gas 1 oven for 2 hours.

Baked Crème Caramel

SERVES 4

PREPARATION TIME 2 HOURS 10 MINUTES

COOKING TIME 3 HOURS 15 MINUTES

INGREDIENTS

6 medium eggs
2 medium egg yolks
300 g / 10 ½ oz / 1 ⅓ cups caster
  (superfine) sugar
750 ml / 1 pint 6 fl. oz / 3 cups whole milk
2 tbsp water
1 orange, cut into slices

METHOD

1. Preheat the oven to 150°C (130°C fan) / 300F / gas 2.

2. Whisk together the eggs, egg yolks and half the caster sugar in a mixing bowl. Add the milk, whisking well.

3. Pass through a fine sieve into a jug and set to one side.

4. Combine the remaining sugar with the water in a small saucepan. Cook over a moderate heat, undisturbed, until the sugar dissolves. Cook until a golden caramel forms.

5. Working quickly and carefully, divide the caramel between four individual ramekins, coating their bases with the caramel.

6. Allow it to cool and settle a little, then place them in a slow cooker. Fill the ramekins with the custard from the jug and pour hot water into the cooker so that it comes halfway up the sides of the ramekins.

7. Cover the cooker with a lid and cook on low for 2–3 hours until just set and there is a slight wobble to the custards when tapped.

8. Remove from the cooker and chill for 2 hours. Run a warmed knife around the edge of the custards to release them and invert onto serving plates. Garnish with orange slices.

TOP TIP

Use fresh eggs for the best taste in these caramels.

Banana and Blueberry Bread

SERVES 8

PREPARATION TIME 15 MINUTES

COOKING TIME 2 HOURS 45 MINUTES

INGREDIENTS

150 g / 5 oz / ⅔ cup margarine, softened
150 g / 5 oz / ⅔ cup caster (superfine) sugar
150 g / 5 oz / 1 cup plain (all-purpose) flour
1 tsp baking powder
½ tsp bicarbonate of (baking) soda
a pinch of salt
2 large eggs
2 small, very ripe bananas, mashed
225 g / 8 oz / 2 cups blueberries
blueberry jam (jelly), to serve

METHOD

1. Beat together the margarine, caster sugar, flour, baking powder, bicarbonate of soda, salt and egg in a mixing bowl for around 3 minutes until pale and smooth.

2. Add the bananas and beat briefly to incorporate, then fold the blueberries through the mixture.

3. Grease and line a 900 g / 2 lb loaf tin with greaseproof paper and fill with the batter.

4. Sit the tin in a slow cooker and cover it with kitchen foil. Cover the slow cooker with a lid.

5. Cook on low for 1 hour, then increase to high and cook for a further 1 hour 30–45 minutes until a cake tester comes out clean from its centre and the top is lightly browned.

6. Remove the tin from the slow cooker and leave to cool on a wire rack.

7. Once cool, turn out the bread, slice and serve with blueberry jam.

TOP TIP

Overripe, blackened bananas make for the best loaf.

Baked Cheesecake

SERVES 8

PREPARATION TIME 15 MINUTES

COOKING TIME 2 HOURS 45 MINUTES

INGREDIENTS

175 g / 6 oz / 1 ¼ cups digestive biscuits, crushed

75 g / 2 ½ oz / ⅓ cup butter, melted

600 g / 1 lb 5 oz / 3 cups cream cheese, softened

300 g / 10 ½ oz / 1 ⅓ cups caster
    (superfine) sugar

150 g / 5 oz / ⅔ cup sour cream

2 large eggs, beaten

2 tbsp lemon juice

2 tsp vanilla extract

300 g / 10 ½ oz / 1 ½ cups frozen raspberries

65 g / 2 ½ oz / ½ cup icing (confectioners')
    sugar, sifted

METHOD

1. Pulse together the crushed biscuits and melted butter in a food processor.

2. Pack the mixture into the base of a 20 cm (8 in) springform cake tin and spread it out evenly with the back of a tablespoon, then chill until ready to use.

3. Preheat the oven to 190°C (170°C fan) / 375F / gas 5.

4. Beat together the cream cheese, sugar, sour cream, eggs, half the lemon juice and the vanilla extract for 3 minutes.

5. Pour the mixture onto the chilled crust and tap the tin lightly to release any trapped air bubbles. Line a roasting tray with a towel, then lift the tin into the tray and pour boiling water around the tin to come halfway up its side. Bake for 30 minutes, then reduce the oven to 120°C (100°C fan) / 250F / gas ½ and continue to bake the cheesecake for 2 hours.

6. Remove to a wire rack to cool. Cook the raspberries and icing sugar with 2 tbsp of water and the remaining lemon juice in a saucepan set over a medium heat.

7. Cook until soft and juicy, stirring frequently. Blend in a food processor, pass through a fine sieve and chill.

8. Chill the cooled cheesecake overnight, then turn out, slice and serve with the prepared raspberry coulis.

TOP TIP

When set, the cheesecake should still have a very slight wobble.

Coffee Cake

SERVES **12**

PREPARATION TIME **15 MINUTES**

COOKING TIME **1 HOUR 50 MINUTES**

INGREDIENTS

225 g / 8 oz / ½ cup unsalted butter, softened
325 g / 11 oz / 1 ½ cups granulated sugar
2 large eggs
1 tsp vanilla extract
1 tsp baking powder
300 g / 10 ½ oz / 2 cups plain (all-purpose)
    flour, sifted
1 tsp bicarbonate of (baking) soda
200 g / 7 oz / 1 cup sour cream
4 tsp instant coffee granules
150 ml / 5 fl. oz / ⅔ cup double (heavy) cream
100 g / 3 ½ oz / ⅓ cup golden syrup

METHOD

1. Preheat the oven to 170°C (150°C fan) /
   325F / gas 3.

2. Cream together the butter and sugar in a
   mixing bowl until pale and thick. Beat in the
   eggs, one by one, adding the vanilla extract
   at the same time.

3. Fold through the baking powder, flour,
   bicarbonate of soda and sour cream.

4. Dissolve half the coffee granules in 1 tbsp
   of boiling water.

5. Fold the dissolved coffee into the batter
   until fully incorporated. Spoon the batter
   into a large bundt cake tin.

6. Bake in the oven for 1 hour 20 minutes.
   Test with a toothpick, if it comes out clean,
   it's ready. If not, return to the oven for a
   further 10–20 minutes until done.

7. Remove to a wire rack to cool. Combine the
   remaining coffee granules with the cream
   and golden syrup in a saucepan.

8. Warm over a low heat, until the coffee has
   dissolved evenly. Turn out the cake once cool
   and pour over the icing before serving.

TOP TIP

Replace the
vanilla extract with
coffee extract or
coffee liqueur.

Bread Pudding

SERVES **4**

PREPARATION TIME **35 MINUTES**

COOKING TIME **1 HOUR 20 MINUTES**

INGREDIENTS

150 g / 5 oz / ⅔ cup butter, softened
10 slices of slightly stale white bread
150 g / 5 oz / 1 cup raisins
500 ml / 18 fl. oz / 2 cups whole milk
2 tsp vanilla extract
4 large eggs
100 g / 3 ½ oz / ½ cup caster (superfine) sugar
110 ml / 4 fl. oz / ½ cup double (heavy) cream
500 ml / 18 fl. oz / 2 cups custard, to serve

METHOD

1. Preheat the oven to 150°C (130°C fan) / 300F / gas 2.

2. Spread the butter on one side of each slice of bread and slice diagonally in half.

3. Scatter some of the raisins in the baking dish and cover with a layer of the bread, butter side down.

4. Sprinkle with the remaining raisins, then cover with the rest of the bread, buttered side up.

5. Whisk together the milk, vanilla, eggs, 85 g / 3 oz / ⅓ cup of sugar and the cream. Strain into a jug and pour half over the bread, leaving it to stand for 20 minutes.

6. Pour the remaining milk mixture over the bread and sprinkle the top with the remaining caster sugar.

7. Bake for 1 hour 15–20 minutes until golden on top. Leave to stand for 5 minutes before serving with the custard.

TOP TIP
Two-day old stale bread is perfect for this recipe.

Treacle Sponge

SERVES 4

PREPARATION TIME 15 MINUTES

COOKING TIME 3 HOURS 15 MINUTES

INGREDIENTS

175 g / 6 oz / ¾ cup unsalted butter, softened
75 g / 3 oz / ¼ cup treacle, warmed
1 tbsp fresh breadcrumbs
175 g / 6 oz / 1 cup soft dark brown sugar
3 large eggs
175 g / 6 oz / 1 ¼ cups self-raising flour, sifted
a pinch of salt
2 tbsp whole milk
150 ml / 5 fl. oz / ⅔ cup double (heavy) cream
150 g / 5 oz / ½ cup golden syrup

METHOD

1. Grease four individual pudding basins with a little of the butter.

2. Combine the treacle with the breadcrumbs in a small mixing bowl. Divide between the pudding basins and place the basins in a slow cooker.

3. Beat together the sugar with the remaining butter until pale and fluffy. Beat in the eggs, one by one, then fold in the flour, salt and milk until incorporated.

4. Divide the batter between the basins and pour in enough hot water to come halfway up the sides of the pudding basins.

5. Cover the cooker with a lid and cook the puddings on low for 2–3 hours until set; a cake tester should come out almost clean from their centres when inserted.

6. Combine the cream and golden syrup in a small saucepan. Cook over a moderate heat, stirring, until thickened and syrupy.

7. Remove the puddings from the cooker and invert onto serving plates, serving with the sauce poured over.

TOP TIP

Run a sharp knife around the insides of the basins to loosen the puddings.

Caramel Pears

SERVES 4

PREPARATION TIME 10 MINUTES

COOKING TIME 4 HOURS 15 MINUTES

INGREDIENTS

250 ml / 9 fl. oz / 1 cup water
175 g / 6 oz / ¾ cup golden caster
  (superfine) sugar
1 tsp vanilla extract
4 ripe pears, split in half and cored
250 g / 9 oz / 1 cup chocolate ice cream
1 tsp flaked sea salt

METHOD

1. Combine the water, sugar and vanilla extract in a small saucepan. Cook over a medium heat, stirring briefly, until the sugar has dissolved.

2. Increase the heat and cook the syrup until boiling. Remove from the heat and add the pears.

3. Swirl to coat and pour into a slow cooker. Cover with a lid and cook on a low setting for 4 hours until the pears are very soft.

4. Remove the pears from the slow cooker and fill with scoops of chocolate ice cream.

5. Garnish with a pinch of flaked sea salt before serving.

TOP TIP

Serve the pears with vanilla ice cream for a classic combination.

Poached Peaches

SERVES **4**

PREPARATION TIME **10 MINUTES**

COOKING TIME **3 HOURS 15 MINUTES**

INGREDIENTS

350 ml / 12 fl. oz / 1 ½ cups water
175 ml / 6 fl. oz / ¾ cup dry white wine
110 g / 4 oz / ½ cup caster (superfine) sugar
4 peaches, pitted and sliced
a small bunch of mint

METHOD

1. Combine the water, wine and sugar in a small saucepan. Cook over a low heat, stirring, until the sugar dissolves.

2. Pour into a slow cooker and add the peach slices. Cover the cooker with a lid and cook on low for 3 hours until the peaches are very soft.

3. Strain the cooking liquid into a saucepan and reduce over a high heat until syrupy. Finely chop 2 tbsp of mint leaves and stir into the reduced sauce.

4. Serve the peaches on plates topped with the mint sauce. Garnish with sprigs of mint leaves.

TOP TIP
In a pinch, use canned peach halves and reduce cooking time by 1 hour.

Tomato Chutney

METHOD

1. Heat the oil in a saucepan set over a high heat until hot. Add the onion, mustard seeds, star anise and cinnamon.

2. Fry for 1 minute, then carefully add the sugar and vinegar. Cover with tomatoes, stir well and pour into a slow cooker.

3. Cover with a lid and cook on low for 5–6 hours until the tomatoes are soft.

4. Adjust the seasoning to taste and leave to cool before spooning into a large, sterilized jar. Seal and store in a cool, dark cupboard.

MAKES **1 LARGE JAR**

PREPARATION TIME **10 MINUTES**

COOKING TIME **6 HOURS 10 MINUTES**

INGREDIENTS

1 tbsp sunflower oil
1 small onion, finely chopped
½ tsp mustard seeds
2 star anise
5 cm (2 in) cinnamon stick
1 tbsp caster (superfine) sugar
75 ml / 3 fl. oz / ⅓ cup distilled vinegar
750 g / 1 lb 10 oz / 5 cups vine tomatoes, cored and roughly chopped
salt and freshly ground black pepper

TOP TIP
Stir the chutney every other hour when in the slow cooker.

Mango Chutney

METHOD

1. Combine all the ingredients apart from the coriander in a slow cooker.

2. Cover the cooker with a lid and cook on low for 6 hours, stirring from time to time.

3. Stir in the coriander and adjust the seasoning to taste.

4. Spoon into a large jar, leave to cool and seal well. Chill before serving.

MAKES **1 LARGE JAR**

PREPARATION TIME **10 MINUTES**

COOKING TIME **6 HOURS**

INGREDIENTS

1 tbsp olive oil
1 red chilli (chili), seeded and finely diced
400 g / 14 oz / 2 cups canned pineapple chunks
    in juice
2 large mangoes, pitted and finely diced
1 lime, juiced
75 ml / 3 fl. oz / ⅓ cup distilled vinegar
2 tbsp caster (superfine) sugar
a handful of coriander (cilantro), finely chopped
salt and freshly ground black pepper

TOP TIP
A small, diced pineapple is a fresh alternative to canned pineapple.

Red Onion Relish

METHOD

1. Combine the red onions, chilli, olive oil, sugar and vinegars in a slow cooker.

2. Cover with a lid and cook on a low setting for 8 hours until thick and jammy, stirring from time to time.

3. Season to taste with salt and pepper before leaving to cool. Spoon into sterilized jars and chill before serving.

MAKES **1 LARGE JAR**

PREPARATION TIME **10 MINUTES**

COOKING TIME **8 HOURS**

INGREDIENTS

6 large red onions, sliced
1 red chilli (chili), seeded and diced
2 tbsp olive oil
175 g / 6 oz / 1 cup soft light brown sugar
150 ml / 5 fl. oz / ⅔ cup balsamic vinegar
110 ml / 4 fl. oz / ½ cup red wine vinegar
salt and freshly ground black pepper

TOP TIP

Caster or granulated sugar are fine to use in a pinch.

Cranberry Sauce

MAKES **1 LARGE JAR**

PREPARATION TIME **10 MINUTES**

COOKING TIME **8 HOURS**

INGREDIENTS

1 orange
400 g / 14 oz / 4 cups fresh cranberries
175 g / 6 oz / ¾ cup caster (superfine) sugar
125 ml / 4 ½ fl. oz / ½ cup water

METHOD

1. Pare the zest from the orange with a vegetable peeler and julienne. Halve the orange and juice into a slow cooker, adding the julienned zest.

2. Add the cranberries, sugar and water and stir well.

3. Cover the cooker with a lid and cook on low for 6–8 hours, stirring occasionally, until soft and jammy.

4. Let the cranberry sauce cool before serving.

TOP TIP

Frozen cranberries can be used in this recipe if fresh are unavailable.

Lemon Curd

MAKES 2 SMALL JARS

PREPARATION TIME 10 MINUTES

COOKING TIME 2 HOURS 45 MINUTES

INGREDIENTS

3 lemons, juiced
175 g / 6 oz / ¾ cup caster (superfine) sugar
125 g / 4 ½ oz / ½ cup unsalted butter, cubed
4 medium eggs, beaten

METHOD

1. Combine the lemon juice, sugar and butter in a heatproof bowl that will sit inside the slow cooker. Sit the bowl in the slow cooker and pour in enough hot water to come halfway up the sides of the bowl.

2. Turn the setting on the slow cooker to high and leave the bowl to sit in the water for around 15 minutes, stirring occasionally, until the sugar, butter and lemon juice have dissolved together.

3. Remove the bowl from the slow cooker, leave to cool slightly and set the slow cooker to low.

4. Strain the beaten egg into the heatproof bowl and whisk until well combined.

5. Return the bowl to the slow cooker and cover with a lid. Cook on the low setting for 1 hour 30 minutes – 2 hours until thickened, stirring from time to time.

6. Give the lemon curd a brief whisk before spooning into sterilized jars. Seal and chill before serving.

TOP TIP

Use the juice of 6 limes instead of lemons for lime curd.

Blackcurrant Jam

METHOD

1. Combine all the ingredients in a slow cooker and stir well.

2. Cover with a lid and cook on a low setting for 6–8 hours until very soft and juicy.

3. Purée the mixture in a food processor and pour into sterilized jars. Leave to cool before sealing and chilling.

MAKES 2 LARGE JARS

PREPARATION TIME 10 MINUTES

COOKING TIME 8 HOURS

INGREDIENTS

450 g / 1 lb / 4 cups blackcurrants, washed
175 g / 6 oz / ¾ cup caster (superfine) sugar
100 g / 3 ½ oz / ½ cup fruit pectin
1 lemon, juiced

TOP TIP
Use half blackcurrants and half blackberries for a two-berry version.

Raspberry Jam

METHOD

1. Combine the raspberries, sugar and water in a slow cooker.

2. Stir well, cover with a lid and cook on a low setting for 6–8 hours until the fruit is very soft.

3. Mash well and spoon into sterilized jars. Leave to cool before sealing and storing.

MAKES 2 LARGE JARS

PREPARATION TIME 5 MINUTES

COOKING TIME 8 HOURS

INGREDIENTS

450 g / 1 lb / 3 cups raspberries
450 g / 1 lb / 2 cups granulated sugar
100 ml / 3 ½ fl. oz / ½ cup water

TOP TIP
Add a half glass of prosecco to the slow cooker for a special jam.

Index